A Writer's Guide to Oral Presentations and Writing in the Disciplines

Christine M. Manion

PRENTICE HALL, UPPER SADDLE RIVER, NEW JERSEY 07458

© 2001 by PRENTICE-HALL, INC.
PEARSON EDUCATION
Upper Saddle River, New Jersey 07458

ISBN 0-13-018931-6
Printed in the United States of America

CONTENTS

✐ DISCIPLINE SECTION II: Writing in the Social Sciences 61

✐ DISCIPLINE SECTION III: Writing in the Natural Sciences 89

✐ Discipline Section IV: Writing in Business   107

✐ References   135

✐ List of WD Supplement Boxes

What are The Disciplines?

As a college student, you have heard the term "discipline" used to describe the various courses or areas of classes you take as part of your core education. But what, specifically, does it mean to write in or for these various disciplines?

Let's take it from the beginning: according to *Webster's New World Dictionary* a discipline is "a branch of knowledge or learning." Particular classes or subjects are grouped together as a branch of learning according to things they have in common. For example, English is not necessarily its own discipline, but part of the larger discipline of the humanities, which includes history, literature, languages, philosophy, and religion. The discipline of social sciences includes anthropology, communication, economics, education, political science, psychology, social work, and sociology. The natural sciences discipline includes science, chemistry, biology, engineering, earth sciences, life sciences, physics, and mathematics. These are the three primary disciplines; business is an additional area that will be discussed in detail in this supplement.

Think of each discipline as its own community of scholars. When you take a course within a particular discipline, you are joining this community of teachers and students, and to be successful, you must learn to clearly communicate with these people. Clear communication comes from recognizing and responding to that discipline's particular expectations of written communication—format, language, research sources, and documentation style. As a student taking courses in the various disciplines, you must be prepared to switch gears quickly and respond to these varying expectations correctly. This supplement will help you successfully make this transition between disciplines.

Various writing assignments are discussed in this supplement, with examples of most, according to the discipline in which you are most likely to be assigned that type of writing. However, many of these tasks overlap; therefore, if you don't find a particular type of writing (e.g., abstract) under a particular discipline (e.g., social science), don't give up! Check the index or refer to **WD Box 1** for a listing of the writing assignments and where they are discussed.

Humanities	Social Sciences	Natural Sciences	Business Writing
Expository Essay	Experience Paper	Abstract	Business Letter
Reflection Paper	Case Study	Abstract Summary	Résumé
Book Review	Literature Review (Survey)	Lab Report	Memo
Critical Analysis	Proposal		E-mail
Bibliographic Essay	Journal Article		Short and Long Reports
Annotated Bibliography	Essay Exam		Collaborative Writing
Grant Proposals			

Before we look at the writing in each discipline, it is important to consider **writing contexts** and **document design**. Any variations needed for particular writing will be discussed under the individual Discipline Section. For all your writing assignments, remember to check with your teacher for any specific guidelines or writing expectations.

Writing Context

Every writing assignment, no matter what the discipline, comes with its own context—the reason you are writing it. The context refers to your **_audience_** and your **_purpose_**. Believe it or not, the teacher should not be your only audience and fulfilling a class requirement should not be your only purpose.

Most academic assignments provide these contexts. For example, an assignment may ask you to write for the general public, your school paper, or a scientific journal. Similarly, an assignment may indicate that your paper should inform your audience of something or be a call to action. Always be aware of the writing context—either stated or implied.

AUDIENCE

When considering **_an audience_**, you need to ask yourself specifically, who are they?

> ➤ General age
> ➤ Gender
> ➤ Cultural background
> ➤ Economic background
> ➤ Educational background
> ➤ Race
> ➤ Religion
> ➤ Interests and/or hobbies

However, for most academic writing, four general audiences are used: (1) your classmates, (2) your teacher, (3) the general public, and (4) specialists in a particular field.

(1) When your **_classmates_** are your audience, build on the common ground you already have—your school, the class you are in, the assignment, etc.

(2) When your **_teacher_** is your audience, consider his or her knowledge of your topic and expectations set for the assignment. Don't forget your prior relationship with the teacher and any feedback you have received.

(3) When the **_general public_** is your audience, think of your parents and neighbors. Consider them to be educated with some general knowledge of your topic, but they also may have some misconceptions.

(4) When **_specialists_** are your audience, remember to speak their language. Don't bore them with too many basic or fundamental concepts. Use the jargon of the field and respect their prior knowledge of the topic.

✐ PURPOSE

The most common purposes for formal writing assignments include (1) to inform, (2) to persuade, (3) to inspire, and (4) to entertain.

(1) To inform means to present knowledge or facts.

(2) To persuade means to induce or prevail on others to act or think a certain way.

(3) To inspire means to motivate or produce an emotion or creative effort.

(4) To entertain means to provide pleasure or amusement.

If the purpose is not clearly stated, look for the verbs in the assignment to help you determine the purpose or the goal of the writing task at hand.

DOCUMENT DESIGN BASICS

Think of your document design as the "packaging" of your ideas. If you do not respect your ideas enough to present them in a clear, professional, and polished manner, your reader is less likely to respect them either. Document design includes consideration of the following:

➤ Margins
➤ Fonts
➤ Headings
➤ Lists
➤ Visuals

✐ MARGINS

Most of your writing will be done on 8½" x 11" plain, white paper. The margins for the entire page should be about one inch. Anything smaller than this will make the text appear crowded. Margins larger than this will make the text look like a framed picture on the page. Line spacing is discussed within each Discipline Section.

If your word-processor gives you the option to justify the right-hand margin, choose not to do so. When a text is right-justified, the computer automatically makes adjustments so that every line ends evenly at the right margin. To do this, additional white space is often added within and between sentences, or the white space between words is made smaller. The combination of these adjustments makes the paragraph look uneven and difficult to read. *The paragraph you are reading is right-justified, and not the preferred style.*

✐ FONTS

With the advent of word-processors, fonts have become a means of personal expression within students' papers. **They should not be used this way.** Choose a font that is pretty standard (New York, Times, Bookman, are a few of the most common ones). A normal size font is between 10 and 12 points. Serif fonts (the fonts with "little feet" at the bottom of certain letters such as the font you are reading) are the easiest fonts to read; therefore, they are preferable to non-serif fonts (these fonts look a bit more casual and funky such as Comic Sans used here). If you are writing something with headings or sections, avoid the urge to use too many fonts. Manipulate the size and appearance of one font by italicizing, underlining, and using boldface. Sometimes, two similar fonts compliment each other in longer reports, but usually no more than two standard fonts should be used in academic writing.

Remember, **when YOU** use *too* many FONTS, your **paper could** look **LIKE** a ransom NOTE!

✎ HEADINGS

In a short essay written for a literature or philosophy course, headings are not needed. However, in longer or more complex writing tasks such as research projects, proposals, and reports, headings offer organization.

When determining if you need headings, write a draft of a Table of Contents (even if your final project will not use one) that includes all headings and subheadings. This gives you an idea if you have enough sections to warrant their use. It also helps you make the headings parallel.

Consistency for all headings on the same level is important. All headings are brief and informative, but the style you choose depends on the information you are presenting in your entire paper, not just a given section. For example, if you use a question for one heading (Can Welfare Reform Really Work?) you cannot change this format for the next heading (A Welfare Reform Success Story). All the headings must "match" in format—all phrases, all statements, all gerund (-ing) phrases, or all questions. See **WD Box 2** for samples of types of formats and consistent headings.

```
┌──────────┐
│   WD     │
│   Box    │
│    2     │
└──────────┘
```

Consistent Headings
Phrase Headings
Paper Topic: Welfare Reform
The history of welfare
The need for welfare reform
The specifics of welfare reform
A welfare reform success story

<u>**Statement Headings**</u>
    Paper Topic: Flextime
        Flextime solves scheduling problems
        Flextime promotes employee job satisfaction
        Flextime saves companies money

<u>**Gerund Headings**</u>
    Paper Topic: On-Site Training Programs
        Training Programs Available
        Justifying Costs to the Company
        Implementing New Training Programs

<u>**Question Headings**</u>
    Paper Topic: Corporate Wellness Centers
        Why are wellness centers so popular?
        How much do wellness centers cost?
        How do wellness centers function?

Headings on the same level of organization should be placed and presented in the same format.

    <u>**MAIN HEADING**</u> (all main headings must be left-flush, all caps, underlined, and boldface)

    Subheading (all subheadings must be indented by five spaces, capitalize only the first letter of major words, do not underline or bold)

Headings are usually centered, left-flush, or indented five spaces. Consistency, again, is the key to making these headings look professional and useful. Headings may be highlighted with color, italicizing, boldface, all caps, underlining, or altering the font size. If you are using lower and upper case letters, capitalize only the major words.

Manipulate the white space around a heading as well. The more white space around a heading, the more likely the reader will notice it.

Remember, headings are supposed to draw the reader's attention to a new section, so if there are too many headings using too many variations, you'll defeat this purpose.

✐ LISTS

The bulleted list has become a crutch for many writers: they list things rather than take the time to write full sentences and paragraphs. In academic writing, lists should be used sparingly. When you use them, do so correctly.

The following types of lists are appropriate in academic writing:

- Recommendations
- Checklists
- Agendas
- Materials
- Instructions

(Note how the preceding information is offered in a bulleted list for your convenience because the items are of equal value and do not need to be discussed in greater detail.)

Guidelines for Bulleted Lists:

1. Indent the bulleted list.
2. Capitalize each item being bulleted.
3. Type the list single-spaced with one blank line preceding and following the list as a whole. If any item in the list requires more than one typed line, leave a blank line between all items in the list.
4. Align any turnovers with the first word in the line directly above it. However, if there is only one item in the list that requires more than one typed line, place it as the last item.
5. Use periods after each item only if each item is an independent clause, a long phrase, or after short phrases essential to the grammatical completeness of the statement introducing the list.
6. Do not use periods after short phrases in a bulleted list if the introductory statement is grammatically complete or the listed items are more of an inventory (shopping list). Do not need use a period after the last item to end the list or the introductory statement. The blank line serves as the separation between the list and the next sentence.
7. Use parallel structure within the bulleted items. Either use all sentences or all clauses, but not a mixture. Be consistent with tense, person, and use of articles.
8. Use the semicolon between items for more formal writing.

✐ VISUALS

Visuals, including charts, graphs, diagrams (illustrations), tables, photographs, and maps are an excellent way to convey complex information and data in a clear and concise format using only a limited space. You may incorporate them directly into your report or proposal or add them as exhibits or appendices at the end of your document.

Thanks to advanced computer programs, it is becoming easy for students to turn data into convenient visuals for the reader. If you choose to use a visual from another source (such as a CD-ROM encyclopedia), you are responsible for giving proper credit for the material in the appropriate documentation style according to the assignment.

Use a visual to contribute, illustrate, or clarify a point already made in the text. However, if it is not discussed, save the visual for an appendix. Within the text, introduce the visual with a complete sentence and provide a commentary after it. Try not to crowd the page. If the page layout seems cramped, save the visual for an appendix.

Guidelines for labeling and placement of visuals may vary according to academic discipline. Refer to each Discipline Section for these specific rules. When deciding how and when to incorporate visuals into your project, keep your readers in mind, as shown in **WD Box 3**.

WD Box 3

Remember Your Audience When Creating Visuals

✓ We read left to right and top to bottom.

✓ We think whatever you place in the center is more important than the things you place on the sides.

✓ We notice the foreground more than the background.

✓ We assume larger objects take precedence over smaller objects.

✓ We see thick lines easier than thin lines.

✓ We tend to group items together that appear to have things in common—pattern, color, shapes, or sizes.

✓ We appreciate contrast in size, shape, and color.

✓ We only value the visuals we understand.

The Oral Report

In conjunction with a written assignment or as a separate assignment, students may have to deliver an oral presentation. How well this is done is often directly related to how well you prepare a written outline or notes.

✐ THE WRITING COMPONENT

Before you can pass a message along to others, it must be clear in your own mind. The best way to know what you want to say is to write it down! Therefore, writing becomes an essential part of preparing for your speech. First, brainstorm a topic, analyze your audience, and create a thesis statement. Then, take good research notes, develop an organizational outline, and draft an introduction and conclusion. Finally, prepare a presentation outline or index cards.

Throughout these stages, writing helps you: 1) to distance yourself from the ideas and remain objective, 2) to pay attention to words and language, and 3) to polish for clarity and impact.

General Purpose
↓
Topic
↓
Audience Analysis
↓
Specific Purpose
↓
Working Thesis
↓
Research Strategy
↓
Organization
↓
Delivery Considerations
↓
Visual Aids
↓
Practice

General Purpose

Usually you will be assigned the purpose of your speech—to inform, to persuade, to inspire, or to entertain. In the academic setting, to inform and to persuade are the most common purposes. *To inform* is to create understanding in your audience. *To persuade* is to influence the attitudes and behaviors of your audience.

Topic

Usually, your topic is assigned. However, if it is open-ended, be careful with your selection. Select a topic you care about, but one your audience will care about also. Choose one that you either already know a lot about or can learn a lot about in the time you have to prepare. Make sure your topic can be handled well within the time constraints of the presentation itself.

Audience Analysis

When determining how best to approach your topic, **_consider your audience_** and adapt your message accordingly.

In the **_classroom setting_**, audience analysis is simple—your classmates and your teacher. However, don't forget them! Ask yourself the following questions: *What year are most of the students (freshmen, seniors)? Are they traditional students? Commuters? Adult learners? Do you all attend a state school? Private school? In this a general education class or a course designed for upper classmen with a particular major?*

In a more **_formal or unfamiliar setting_**, don't make assumptions or stereotypes to analyze your audience. If you've been asked to speak to a group, ask whoever arranged your speech about your specific audience. Gather information as to the occasion, other speakers, the time limit, and the size of the audience. If possible, talk to some of the members of the audience before your speech (and thank them in your speech), or if there is time, use a questionnaire to gather pertinent information and refer to your findings in your presentation. These steps help you stay audience-focused during your presentation, and add to your credibility.

Think of **_knowledge_** of your topic as a staircase. On what step would you place your message? On what step would you place the audience's knowledge? To determine the audience's placement, ask yourself: *How much does my audience already know about this topic? What terms and concepts will they not know? What steps must I provide as a foundation for my message?*

Informed Audience:

Don't waste their time with the basics, but introduce new ideas and concepts. From the beginning, reassure them that you will be covering new ground.

Uninformed Audience:
Limit the number of new ideas you try to present. Use visual aids to establish the basics, avoiding technical jargon whenever possible. Define new terms and concepts. Repeat key ideas and use vivid examples.

Mixed Audience:
Start with the simple concepts and move toward the more complex ones. In the introduction, acknowledge the presence of the more informed members of the audience and explain how you will only begin with the basics so that everyone is "on the same page."

When you *adapt* your presentation to the general needs and expectations of your audience, that does not mean catering to them and only saying what they want to hear. It simply means considering their knowledge levels and interests in order to make your message relevant by using appropriate language and examples. This maximizes their chances of connecting with your message.

Specific Purpose
The specific purpose of your speech should be written as an infinitive phrase (to inform, to convince, to show). It should narrow your topic to one main point using specific terms and precise language that can be achieved in the time constraints of the assignment.

Working Thesis
Your working thesis pulls together the general purpose, audience analysis, and specific purpose. Just like a thesis in an essay, it is a *roadmap* for the listeners. It promises them a destination. In preparing your speech, it is also a practical preparation step because it helps you narrow your topic, it introduces and connects the key concepts of your presentation, and it is a catalyst for your research.

State your sub-headings (two to five points that will support your main message) as sign posts for the listeners. Don't forget that this is only a *working thesis*, and it will need to be rewritten when your research and outline are complete. In your final thesis statement, avoid using a process statement ("Today I will discuss" or "In this presentation, I will offer"). Instead, make an assertion about your topic.

A thesis statement in an oral report often feels contrived and rehearsed. That's okay. Unlike the reading experience in which the active reader may reread and contemplate a statement before moving on, the listening experience demands the obvious be stated so that even the laziest listener is ready to move on when your speech does.

General Purpose	Topic	Specific Purpose	Working Thesis
To inform	Infertility	To explain medical advancements in the treatment of infertility	The sorrow of infertility is becoming a thing of the past for many couples thanks to medical procedures such as donor insemination, invitro fertilization, and egg harvesting.

Research Strategy

When you receive an oral report assignment, divide the preparation into manageable tasks according to a realistic timeline. Set small goals and stick to your calendar in order to give yourself enough time to research, organize, and practice your presentation.

Research should go from *__general to specific information__*. Investigate the big picture before you look for perfect illustrations, examples, or statistics for your speech. Cater your research to the determined needs and interests of your audience. Use the library and sources specific to the area of study (listed under each discipline section in this supplement). If your topic is a current event or particularly timely, avoid outdated books. Be careful with the Internet and check for the credibility of the sources.

To Note or Not to Note?
➤ Skim the material.
Look at headings, the first and last paragraphs.
Determine if this is worthwhile to read in full.
➤ If yes, reread the material carefully.
➤ Summarize the key points in a few sentences (not phrases or words).
➤ Use direct quotations when the information is particularly well stated.
➤ Take more notes than you need.

Note Taking:
➤ Use Index Cards.
➤ Divide them into **Source cards** and **Information cards**.
Use source cards to keep track of each source's biographical information.
Use information cards to take notes.

> Use only one side of each card.
> Write only one fact on each card.
> Carefully label the source and page number for each information card.
> Carefully label if you are quoting or paraphrasing each piece of information.

Organization

Stick to the timeline to stop researching; otherwise, students over-research and then find themselves rushed to organize and practice the presentation.

Once you have your index cards, lay them out in front of you and survey everything you have compiled. Identify the information you will use and stack them together into the major subheadings of your speech. Always work on the body of your speech first (supporting material). Experiment with the order of this material a few times. When you think you have the best order, create an organizational outline.

Organizational Outline:
> This is for organization only and NOT to use for your final speech.
> Use major headings with two to three subheadings and a consistent numbering system.
> Use sentences for your main points to sharpen your thinking as you draft.

TITLE OF SPEECH

General Purpose: _____

Topic: _____

Specific Purpose: _____

Thesis: _____

Introduction

   A. _____

   B. _____

(transition)

Supporting Material

   A. _____

      1._____

      2._____

(transition)

   B. _____

      1._____

      2._____

(transition)

C. _____

    1. _____

    2. _____

(transition)

Conclusion

    A. _____

    B. _____

    C. _____

Introduction:

Answer these questions for the audience immediately—*Who are you? What are your qualifications? What are you going to talk about? Why should they listen?*

➤ Grab your audience's attention with a question, quotation, fascinating statistic, anecdote, background information, or compliment.

➤ Give your audience a "road map" so that they will always know where you are, where you are going, when you are there, and what they have to look forward to.

➤ Explain your organization so they may follow along.

➤ Write your introduction last.

Supporting Materials:

The longer your presentation, the more likely your audience will become bored or restless. Organization keeps things moving on the right path.

➤ Give signals to show where you are on the roadmap. Use *first, second,* and *third* appropriately. Show cause and effect with words such as *subsequently, therefore,* and *furthermore.* If you're telling a story, use signposts such as *before, then,* and *next.*

➤ Define unfamiliar terms and give vivid examples to help the audience understand these new ideas and concepts.

➤ Add narratives, examples, and testimonies only if they are relevant to the audience and to your topic.

➤ Use statistics carefully, responsibly, and fairly.

➤ Comment on your own materials. Tell the audience what is significant, memorable, or relevant—and why.

➤ Repeat key ideas. Do so sparingly, but emphatically in order to emphasize the importance of the idea and to help the audience remember it.

➤ Draw on authorities, but don't name drop.

➤ Provide internal summaries. Take a moment to occasionally recap what you have covered as reassurance for both yourself and your audience.

Conclusion:

Always make the conclusion lively and memorable and offer the audience the sense of closure they look for, the summary they need, and the reinforcement of the thesis they appreciate.

➤ Signal the end with verbal ("in conclusion") and non-verbal (facial expressions, gestures) cues.
➤ Offer a fresh restatement of your main message.
➤ Use a clincher: state a quote, issue a challenge, or give an illustration.
➤ When you say "finally," make sure you mean it!
➤ Draft and redraft this important final impression.

> **WD**
> **Box**
> **4**

Introduction and Conclusion Don'ts

Introduction Don'ts

✓ Don't say "Before I begin" because you already have!
✓ Don't apologize for being nervous, unprepared, etc.
✓ Don't read an introduction.
✓ Don't use a dramatic opener that has no connection to your topic.
✓ Don't make the introduction too long.

Conclusion Don'ts

✓ Don't drag out the conclusion.
✓ Don't conclude more than once.
✓ Don't end on a weak or rambling note.
✓ Don't introduce new points.

Delivery Considerations

Presentation Styles:

1. **Memorization.** This approach works if you need to give the presentation a number of times (a tour guide scenario). Otherwise, if you forget a single word, you are in danger of losing the remainder of the speech. Be careful with memorized speeches because sometimes they sound mechanical.

2. **Reading.** This form of presenting your materials is appropriate when you cannot afford to deviate from exactly what has been prepared. This presentation style could bore audiences and create an uncomfortable barrier between you and your audience. Therefore, if you must read

your materials, remember to make eye contact with your audience often, use inflections for emphasis, and use appropriate gestures to add "life" into the speech.

3. **Extemporaneous.** This style of presentation is usually your best bet. You are well prepared and reading from an outline or index cards, not a speech. This outline contains the major points you want to make, but the language is of the moment rather than memorized.

Presentation Outline:
This is to be used to give an extemporaneous speech following the same style as the preparation outline, but with some additions and some deletions.

➤ Type the outline in all caps for easier reading.
➤ Clearly indicate the introduction, supporting material, and conclusion.
➤ Use key words and phrases only or you'll end up reading from a script.
➤ Put in cues for pauses, use of visuals, or emphasis.
➤ Use single-sided paper so there is less shuffling of paper.
➤ Highlight key points you cannot afford to skip.
➤ Prepared transitions.
➤ Follow the outline!

Presentation Index Cards:
➤ Number or label the order of the index cards.
➤ Use one index card per fact.
➤ Use one side of each index card only.
➤ Use various colors of pen on white cards or different card colors to separate topics or segments of your speech.
➤ Write clearly in all caps.
➤ Highlight key points that you cannot afford to skip—small sticky notes are good for this.
➤ If visuals are used with your speech, clearly indicate when to use them on the card PRIOR to the one with the explanation of the visual.

Language:
By drafting an introduction, a preparation outline, and a conclusion, you are able to carefully consider the general language of your presentation, which must be Correct, Clear, and Concrete.

Correct Words:
Recognize the power of the perfect word
"Never in the **field of human conflict** was so much owed by so many to so few." Winston Churchill

Notice the change in impact when "field of human conflict" is changed to "history": "Never **in history** was so much owed by so many to so few." It just doesn't sound as powerful nor as memorable!

Recognize the power of the offensive word
If there's any chance a word, phrase, or example could offend anyone in your audience, don't use it.
Avoid sexist nouns and pronouns.

Recognize the power of using the proper word

Allusion versus illusion	Irregardless (not a word)
Affect versus effect	Anyways (not a word)

Recognize the power of misspoken grammar

Between you and I (wrong)	Between you and me (correct)
I had wrote it (wrong)	I wrote it or I had written it (correct)

Clarity of Meaning:

Denotation versus Connotation
Denotation refers to a dictionary definition usually affected by the culture and the age.
Connotation refers to the emotional definition (what people associate with the word). It can be more powerful than the denotation.

For example, **inexpensive** usually has positive connotations, but **cheap** has negative connotations.

Don't use redundancies for emphasis

1 a.m. in the morning	brief moment
at this point in time	first and foremost

Use the active voice for fewer words in sentences
Gun control is an issue that must be considered by all citizens. (Passive)
All citizens must consider the issue of gun control. (Active)

Avoid clichés
Better be safe than sorry!
No pain, no gain!

Avoid nominals
We then **had a discussion** about the Supreme Court's decision. (nominal)

We **discussed** the Supreme Court's decision. (strong verb)

Avoid substitute subjects
There are four issues I will present today.
I will present four issues.

Concrete Language:

Use specific details
Say "Toni Morrison" instead of "a writer."

Use guide phrases
Now, first, my next point, etc.

Use visual imagery
Include similes such as "the snow covered the field like a fresh white blanket."
Include metaphors such as "education is an exciting journey."
Don't mix metaphors such as "you'll be up the creek without a parachute," which should read "you'll be up the creek without a paddle."

Verbal Communication:

Your voice is the focus of the presentation, so be aware of it. This does not mean you have to shout, but project. If you are using a microphone, don't raise your voice, and don't "eat" the microphone either. Articulate, speak slowly and deliberately, but not so slowly that there is no rhythm or pace to the speech. Change the tone of your voice for emphasis and clarity. Insert planned pauses. In general, sound like yourself, but an intensified version.

Non-Verbal Communication:

Your body language will either add or detract from your overall message. Eye contact is the most important non-verbal communication tool; therefore, make eye contact with your audience immediately. If walking up to a podium, don't begin speaking before you've gotten there, squared off, and looked directly at the audience. Your eyes communicate confidence, so don't look over their heads to a back wall.

Facial expressions should mirror the various appropriate emotions of your message. Your posture should be straight, but not stiff. *Take your hands out of your pockets!* Rest them on the podium, but don't grip the podium, lean on the desk, or lounge against a back wall or chalkboard. Your gestures should be natural—don't force them. Use them for emphasis. Try not to primp or fidget out of nervousness. Body movements should be kept to a minimum, and used in pace with the speech. Step forward or backward to indicate transitions, but don't sway side to side. Of course, dress appropriately.

Visual Aids

Visual aids should make ideas clear and understandable, but they should not take the place of a well-prepared speech. They add interest to an already interesting topic. They reinforce key ideas by providing illustrations or concrete images for the audiences, and if done well, they can make long explanations unnecessary. Visuals can also be excellent devices for ESL listeners and add to your credibility.

```
WD
Box
5
```

Visual Aids Do's:

✓ Design them large enough for entire audience to see
✓ Design them simply and clearly
✓ Design them for maximum impact

Visual Aids Don'ts:

✓ Don't use too much text
✓ Don't use excessive artwork
✓ Don't make a page look cramped
✓ Don't use too many colors
✓ Don't overuse all caps

Posters and Erase Boards. Pre-made posters are great because they are unobtrusive during the report. If they are in front of the audience during your entire speech, but you only refer to them at various moments, you may want to cover them so they don't distract from your presentation or lose their impact.

Erase boards are preferable to chalkboards because their colors are visually appealing. They are good for the occasional technical word (for spelling and as a memory aid), but don't write complicated graphs during your speech or your audience will become fascinated with this process and not with what you are saying. Also, people tend to make mistakes when writing in front of an audience.

Slides. If you are using slides, create them specifically for your presentation. Don't use slides from graphs drawn for your original paper. The quality of these reproductions is usually questionable. Before your speech, make sure the slides are in the proper order, placed in the machine in an upright position (upside-down slides will get the audience's attention, but they don't do much for your professional reputation). Double-check that the slide projector is working, focused, and if the screen you will be using won't be up for your entire presentation, make sure you know how to get it up and down easily.

Transparencies. If you are using overheads, dim the lights in the hall—do not turn them completely off. Despite their best efforts, some members of your audience may drift off to sleep! Have your overhead sheets in the proper order and easily accessible before you begin your presentation. Label the sheets—sticky notes are good for this. Before your speech, double-check the focus of the overhead projector, its distance from the screen, the accessibility of the screen, and how to place the sheets on the projector so they appear correctly on the screen. Backward and upside-down images are enough to undermine the confidence of even a seasoned speaker.

PowerPoint. If you are making a PowerPoint presentation, the most important thing to do is double-check the system before you begin. If possible, bring your own laptop just in case the software or computer is not compatible with the disk you have brought. PowerPoint technology can be an amazing addition to your presentation, but remember, it is only an enhancement. Your information—spoken with clarity and authority—is the main attraction.

Handouts. Do not distribute complicated handouts during your presentation. A handout that is too detailed distracts the audience from what you are saying. When you are distributing short and simple handouts during the speech, try not to speak about the handouts until everyone has one. Similarly, don't distribute the handout before you are ready to discuss it.

Unexpected Problems with Visual Aids:
Be prepared for a worst-case scenario. Visuals are excellent tools, but if need be, you should be able to give your presentation without them. If something goes noticeably wrong during your presentation, relax. It happens to everyone! Simply take a deep breath, give an appropriate apology to the audience (if necessary), and keep going.

Summary for Using Visuals:
➤ Use visuals when practicing your presentation.

- Don't talk to the visual, but to the audience.
- Don't let visuals distract from your speech.
- Don't use too many visuals.
- Be careful with typos and spelling errors as they look HUGE on a big screen.
- Don't rely on them too heavily as things could go wrong.

Practice

When planning your timeline, give yourself enough time for at least four complete run-throughs of your entire presentation (using visuals). When you practice, keep the following in mind:

- Practice ideas rather than words or you will try to memorize things.
- Time yourself and edit or expand accordingly.
- Walk through the entire speech and note places that are problematic, but wait to fix them until later.
- Practice in front of a mirror, on videotape, or in front of a friend. Ask that friend for constructive feedback, including: *What was my main point? Did the points flow? Did any information seem to come from out of nowhere or not fit in with the information around it? Did I sound natural? Did I look natural? How did the visuals add to my message?*
- Practice your introduction and conclusion a few extra times.
- Don't add too much on the outline or each index card during your practice sessions.

Question and Answer

If there will be a Question and Answer period, be ready for it. Embrace the Q&A period by anticipating questions and practicing answers. When you first open the floor for questions, there may be an awkward silence—that's okay. Be prepared to fill it with prompts or questions of your own.

The key to a successful Q&A session is to *stay in control.* This means jumping in on long-winded speechmakers and moving to another audience member. If someone has a number of follow-up questions after you've answered the first question, thank him or her, explain the time constraints, and move on. If someone seems ready to pick a fight, stay diplomatic. Simply turn it around to your advantage and move on. Decline to answer a question if you consider it inappropriate.

Q&A etiquette is quite simple. Always look directly at the person asking the question as a sign of respect. If you're in a large room, repeat the question so everyone hears it before you begin your answer. Try not to praise one question as the other people asking questions will notice you did not do this for their question. If you don't know an answer, admit it. If someone brings up an error you've made, don't be defensive. If you've misspoken, apologize, correct it, and move on. Have a time limit and stick to it.

Nerves

If you suffer from stage fright, don't worry; you can turn this nervous energy to good use during your speech. The more prepared and rehearsed you are, the less frightened you will be. Remember—knowledge is power. Practice your introduction more because that's when you will be most nervous. Plan to use good visual aids to take the attention off yourself. Check the arrangements before hand to build your confidence.

Think of the speech as communication, not performance!

The physical signs of anxiety strike different people in different ways, but most can be abated:

➤ Pounding heart: Don't worry. No one else can hear it!
➤ Trembling hands: Rest them on the podium. If there's no podium, place one in one pocket and grip the lapel of your jacket with the other.
➤ Shaky knees: Stand behind the desk or podium. If there's no desk, step forward and backward for emphasis.
➤ Dry throat/mouth: Keep water at the podium and remember it's okay to take an occasional sip.
➤ Quivering voice: It fades quickly, but until it does, add volume.
➤ Flushed face: It's not as noticeable as you think, and it will fade as the speech proceeds.

Remember, to act confident is to appear confident is to become confident!

When you step up to speak, stop. Count to five. Take a deep breath. Look at the audience. Don't expect to see smiling faces, and begin. If you've prepared a well-organized and thought provoking speech, the audience will only notice the message. Some might say that to be overly self-conscious or shy in front of an audience is an indication that you have quite an ego! Stop thinking that the audience is there to critique how you look or the tone of your voice. That's just the packaging of the message. So get over yourself and concentrate on delivering the message!

Discipline Section I: Writing in the Humanities

The *humanities* encompass a variety of subjects, including art, history, literature, music, languages, philosophy, and religion. The foundation of these subjects is defined as "the branch of learning concerned with human thought and relations, as distinguished from the sciences." The humanities concentrate on the human experience and interpretation of that experience; therefore, writing in the humanities presents persuasive and convincing explications of facts, observations, and occurrences.

✐ PRIMARY VERSUS SECONDARY SOURCES

Primary sources are original documents, such as a novel, a speech, a diary, congressional records, field research, lab reports, and eyewitness accounts. **Secondary sources** comment upon primary sources.

For example, in a literature class the primary source would be the novel or story you are discussing (The Color Purple by Alice Walker). You may be asked to write a critical analysis based on only the primary source. This means you write a thoughtful analysis of an aspect of the novel using quotations from the novel itself to support your interpretations. However, if you are asked to support your interpretations with secondary sources, you must research appropriate scholarly journals and books for discussions about The Color Purple, and then smoothly integrate those particular ideas that support your analysis into your own paper.

✐ RESEARCH SOURCES

Part of writing good papers that incorporate both primary and secondary sources is being able to find those sources. Therefore, library research plays an integral part of the writing projects required in most of your humanities subjects. The most obvious place to start your research is the Humanities Index. This general source of information lists articles from over 200 scholarly journals in areas such as history, language, literary criticism, and religion. It is available both in hard copy and online.

After looking at that general source of information, you may want to consult the following sources according to the subject you are studying.

Titles followed by an asterisk (*) indicate that the source also comes in some sort of electronic format (website, CD-ROM, online database, etc.). Always check with your librarian to see what is available to you.

History

America: History and Life (United States)*
Cambridge Ancient History
Cambridge Medieval History
CRIS (Combined Retrospective Index to Journals in History, 1838–1974)
Dictionary of American History
Encyclopedia of Latin American History and Culture
Great Events in History

Guide to Historical Literature (AHA)
Harvard Guide to American History
Historical Abstracts (Europe)*)
New Cambridge Modern History

Language and Literature

Annual Bibliography of English Language and Literature*
Biography Index*
Book Review Digest*
Book Review Index
Cassell's Encyclopaedia of World Literature
Children's Literature Abstracts
Children's Literature Review
Contemporary Authors*
Current Biography*
Dictionary of Literary Biography*
Essay and General Literature Index*
European Writers
Language and Language Behavior Abstracts (LLBA)*

Literary History of the United States (LHUS)
MLA International Bibliography*
Oxford Companion to American Literature
Oxford Companion to Classical Literature
Oxford Companion to English Literature
Oxford English Dictionary (OED)
New Princeton Encyclopedia of Poetry and Poetics
PMLA General Index
Reference Guide to Short Fiction
Salem Press Critical Surveys of Poetry, Fiction, Long Fiction, and Drama
Twentieth Century Authors
Webster's Biographical Dictionary
World Literature Criticism

Philosophy

The Concise Encyclopedia of Western Philosophy and Philosophers
Dictionary of the History of Ideas
Encyclopedia of Philosophy
Oxford Companion to Philosophy
Philosopher's Index*

Religion

Encyclopedia of Ethics
Encyclopaedia of Judaica

The Hutchinson Encyclopedia of Living Faiths
New Catholic Encyclopedia

Encyclopaedia of Islam
Encyclopedia of Religion

Oxford Dictionary of the Christian Church
Religion Index*

Non-Library Sources

Other important information in the humanities disciplines may be found through interviews, archival searches, courthouse records, documents kept at city hall, or actual visits to particular sites of interest.

Although the Internet can provide easy access to other universities and colleges around the world, there is also a lot of misinformation floating around out there. Ultimately, each teacher has the final word as to whether or not Internet sources are allowed for any given research assignment.

✐ WRITING EXPECTATIONS IN THE HUMANITIES

Assignments for writing in the humanities require you to exercise your **abstract, historical, and critical thinking skills**. Abstract thinking considers an idea or concept presented—both at close range and from a distance—as practiced in philosophy, linguistics, and religion. Historical thinking examines cause and effect, and traces the development or evolution of peoples, nations, ideas, or even fashions, as found in history courses. Critical thinking analyzes, interprets, and evaluates the world of "texts," including books, poetry, and drama, as well as films, musical scores, paintings, and sculpture as studied in writing, literature, and art classes. Depending on the subject and the level of the class (freshman versus upper-level), you may be asked to respond and write using one, two, or all three of these kinds of thinking skills.

Because of the particular topics unique to the humanities, the writing, presentation, and **language** may be less formal than that found in the social and natural sciences. However, clarity of ideas remains essential to writing in the humanities. Writing in the first person (I) may be acceptable for personal papers or narratives, but the third person (they) is used for most research papers.

✐ ORGANIZATIONAL PATTERNS IN THE HUMANITIES

The organizational pattern for a paper establishes the way it approaches the topic—the writing strategy. The most common pattern for organizing a paper written in the humanities presents an idea, interpretation, event, or detail and then thoroughly explains and supports that idea or interpretation in a thoughtful and carefully considered way. The paper should present its discussion in the logical order introduced in its thesis statement or introduction.

Transitional sentences and words are used to show how the paper is organized rather than headings or sections.

The various patterns or strategies are sometimes referred to as "modes" or methods of writing. The organization of your paper is often determined by the assignment: analyze, compare/contrast, define, etc. See **WD Box 6** for a detailed listing of these strategies.

✐ DOCUMENT DESIGN BASICS FOR THE HUMANITIES

The general principles covered under **Document Design Basics** regarding margins and fonts should be followed for most of the writing you will do in these courses, but always clarify expectations regarding use of technical jargon and appropriateness of using first (I) or third (they) person in the paper.

The humanities paper is a single unit in which all the paragraphs are connected to a thesis and to one another. Longer research papers may include headings and abstracts, but that would be the exception and not the rule.

The following shows the traditional style sources used for each subject within the humanities discipline:

Literature and Language
MLA Handbook for Writers of Research Papers (5th edition)

History, Philosophy, Religion
The Chicago Manual of Style (14th edition)
A Manual for Writers of Term Papers, Theses, and Dissertations. Ed. Kate L. Turabian (6th edition)

This section offers an overview of both the MLA and the CMS formats and expectations (Turabian follows the CMS guidelines).

MLA: Title Page
Most papers in the humanities do not require a title page. The title, author, class, and date are provided on the first page of the text instead. Papers are normally double-spaced, using five space indents to indicate new paragraphs (no extra lines are needed).

*See the following example and the **MLA sample paper** at the end of this section:*

Your Name   Last name 1

Your Teacher's Name

The Course Name and Number

The Date

                    Title of the Paper (centered, do not underline)

    Indent each paragraph by five spaces, double space between lines, and do not add

any additional lines between paragraphs. For longer quotes (four or more lines of text

or three or more lines of poetry), block indent the entire quotation one inch (about ten

spaces) and do not use quotation marks. Put your last name followed by the page

number in the upper right corner of each page using arabic numbers (1,2,3, etc.)

without periods or parentheses.

MLA: Visuals

For MLA papers, visuals are either **Tables or Figures** (including charts, graphs, illustrations, maps, and photographs). **Tables** are labeled by arabic numerals without a period:

Table 1   Table 2

This label should appear on a separate line above the table, flush left, and a brief caption identifying the subject of the table appears on the line below the label. Capitalize the caption as though it were a title.

For **figures**, both the label and the caption follow the figure, and they do not have to be on separate lines. The labels may be written out or abbreviated:

Figure 6   Fig. 14

If the **table or figure** is borrowed from another source, give the source information below the table, left-flush, double-spaced using proper MLA internal citation format.

The visuals may appear in the text or as part of a separate appendix following the paper.

Example of MLA table:

Table 6

Sample MLA Table with Title

	Food	**Gas**	**Motel**
Jan	12	17	10
Feb	17	11	21
Mar	22	29	14
Apr	14	10	17

Example of MLA figure:

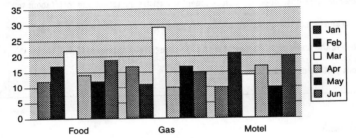

Figure 3. Citation Source, by Author, Publisher (pg #).

This caption is double-spaced and left-flush with the regular margins for the paper, and not adapted to the size of the table or figure.

MLA: Documentation of Visuals

Chart, Graph, Table, Map

On the Works Cited page of an essay, a table, map, chart, or graph is cited like a book with an unknown author. Underline the title of the visual and follow it with the appropriate noun (chart, graph, table, map).

Medieval Germany and Italy. Map. New Jersey: Prentice-Hall, Inc., 1994.

Photograph, Cartoon

On the Works Cited page of an essay, a photograph or cartoon is listed alphabetically by the cartoonist's or photographer's last name, followed by the title (if it has one), the word "cartoon" or "photograph" and the publication information from which the visual was taken.

Meiselas, Susan. "Guerrilla in El Salvador, 1983." Photograph. Benjamin Keen and Mark Wasserman, eds. A Short History of Latin America. Boston: Houghton Mifflin, 1984.

CMS: Title Page, Margins and Line Spacing

For CMS format, use a separate title page, and approximately two inches down from the top, type the title of your paper. Capitalize all words except articles and small prepositions. Spaced evenly below this, type your name, then the department and/or teacher's name, and the date (month and year only). On the first page of your text, type the title of your paper again, centered, capitalizing only the major words in the title.

See the following example and the **CMS sample paper** *at the end of this section:*

TITLE of the PAPER

(center, do not underline)

by

Your Name

History Department

April 2000

1

Title of the Paper

Indent each paragraph by five spaces, double-space between lines, and do not add any additional lines between paragraphs. For longer quotes (two or more sentences that run to eight or more lines of text), block indent the entire quotation four spaces from the left margin and single-space the quotation, without any quotation marks.

Put the page number in the upper right corner of each page using arabic numbers (1,2,3, etc.) without periods or parentheses.

CMS: Visuals

For CMS papers, visuals are either labeled as **Tables or Figures** (these include all illustrative materials such as drawings, paintings, photographs, charts, graphs, and maps). Tables are labeled with arabic numerals followed by a period and a title, or the title may appear on the following line. The label is placed directly above the table, left-flush or centered (left-flush if the title follows it, centered if the title appears on the next line):

Table 2. Appropriate Title with Capitalization of Major Words

Table 2.

Appropriate Title with Capitalization of Major Words

A more traditional label is written in all caps, centered, and the title is centered on the line below:

TABLE 2.

APPROPRIATE TITLE IN ALL CAPS

Whichever style you use, be consistent throughout your paper.

Example of CMS table:

Table 10.
CENSUS OF IRELAND FOR THE YEAR 1851:
Population of County Mayo Baronies

	1841	1851
Burrishoole	39,853	24,752
Carra	52,238	32,707
Clanmorris	27,437	19,782
Costello	48,389	43,217
Erris	26,428	19,632
Gallen	46,566	34,336
Kilmaine	42,342	31,216
Murrisk	34,402	24,992
Tirawley	71,232	44,195
TOTAL	**388,887**	**274,830**

Figures (or illustrations) may appear in the text or as part of a separate appendix following the paper.

Even if your paper contains several kinds of illustrations, label them consistently and consecutively using arabic numerals: Fig. 5   Figure 13

You may follow the label with a title or a caption (also called a legend).
Fig. 8.   Map of Lake Michigan

The caption may consist of one or two sentences of explanation, but they do not necessarily have to be written as complete sentences. The caption should be single-spaced and run the width of the illustration. Shorter captions are centered.

A brief statement of the source, or credit line, is usually appropriate. There is no fixed style for this credit line, but it usually appears at the end of the legend in a smaller font or parentheses. The style should be consistent throughout your paper and reflect similar information as included in a first reference footnotes. Short forms are acceptable if the source is fully listed in the bibliography.

Example of CMS figure:

Figure 1. Map of Ireland
Reprinted from Author, Title (Publisher, date), pg. #.

CMS: Documentation of Visuals

The **documentation of the tables and figures** usually appears as part of the legend of the table or figure itself within the text. If the source of the visual is listed in the bibliography, follow the appropriate rules for whatever type of publication it is (book, journal, anthology, etc.) with no specific mention of the table or figure. In this case, the caption within the text only needs a shortened version of that citation.

✐ ASSIGNMENTS IN THE HUMANITIES

1. The Expository Essay
   Many basic writing courses are called **"expository writing."** In this context, expository refers to writing that presents facts, ideas, or details in order to explain. In other courses, expository essay assignments often omit the word

"expository" and replace it with the particular writing task at hand. These assignments include: to compare and contrast two things or concepts (the causes of WW I versus the causes of WW II); to define a word or concept (multiculturalism); to narrate an event (your first day of college); to argue a point (the universal banning of nuclear testing); to illustrate something (examples of after-death experiences); to classify according to shared characteristics (monosyllabic versus multi-syllabic prefixes and suffixes); to trace the cause-and-effect of an event or trend (the invention of the printing press and the rise of the Protestant Reformation).

These types of assignments are not exclusive to the humanities, and they are very common terms found in essay examinations as well. Therefore, it is worthwhile to become familiar with these terms and the expectations that come along with them.

WD Box 6 contains the most common verbs used in expository writing assignments and essay examinations.

> **WD**
> **Box**
> **6**

Expository Essays

✓ *__Compare & Contrast__:* Explain likenesses and differences between two similar subjects or ideas either point-by-point (moving back and forth between the two ideas) or subject-by-subject (dealing completely with one idea and then dealing completely with the next idea). Your goal is to make a value judgment of which subject or idea is better than the other.

✓ *__Define__:* Explain a topic by closely presenting the meaning of the word or concept in minute detail. Your goal is to clarify by using specifics to illuminate abstractions or generalities.

✓ *__Narrate__:* Explain by telling what is occurring or what has occurred, usually in chronological order. Your goal is to walk the reader through the experience.

✓ *__Argue__:* Explain and persuade by presenting your side of a complex issue using logical reasoning and strong evidence. Your goal is to convince your reader that your side is the most valid option or opinion.

✓ *__Illustrate__:* Explain by using examples or models. Your goal is to offer concrete, specific information that supports the main idea or concept.

✓ **_Classify:_** Explain by showing shared characteristics. Your goal is to justify the organization of grouping items or ideas together in order to analyze them in a logical and coherent manner.

✓ **_Cause-and Effect:_** Explain by examining the origins of an event in relationship to the results of it. Your goal is to show the connection between the reasons for an outcome and the outcome itself.

2. The Book Review

   A book review asks you to critically assess a book based on a set of standards within a particular field. The goal of your book review is to assess the worth of the text in relation to the context in which a typical reader would be using that book. Avoid giving a play-by-play summary of the action. **A book review is not a book report.** Begin a book review by detailing what the author is attempting to do, including a summary of the key points or arguments presented in the book. Then, evaluate this argument and the supporting evidence provided. You should also address the organization, language, and style in which the information is presented. Conclude the review with your overall critical assessment of the book.

   The following excerpt comes from a book review written for a literature course that asked students to consider older works of fiction as they might be received and reviewed today.

   The novel <u>Pamela</u> by Samuel Richardson, published in 1741, is written in the form of a series of letters. This form of writing, known as epistolary fiction, while not invented by Richardson was perfected by him in this study of moral issues of his time. The work, subtitled "Virtue Rewarded," at first seems to be interested in only one moral issue—a young lady's virtue. Upon closer examination, however, it becomes apparent that there are many moral issues considered in the story's action. The characters in <u>Pamela</u> tend to be divided into three categories of moral issues: sexuality, class, and morality of conscience verses morality of appearance.

3. The Reflection Paper (or Critical Response Statement)

   You may be asked to write a response to something you have read or observed. In this assignment, you are supposed to offer your reactions in a first person account that explore the factors that influenced your response.

The first part of a critical reflection may contain a concise synopsis of the key themes of a lecture or reading or an analytical overview of what was observed. The second part usually offers a sustained analysis of the themes or overview using your own critical questions and insights. Although this is a personal account, use specific details to illustrate your response and explain your reflections. The following sample is taken from a homework journal in which the student is asked to reflect upon a reading assignment using personal anecdotes as well as specific details from the assigned chapter.

Portion of a Reflection Paper from a linguistics class:

After reading the first chapter of <u>The Story of English</u>, I have

already gained respect for the English language and its incredible history. I

had no idea that English did not even exist 2000 years ago, and look how far

we've come! I got very caught up in the section about Shakespeare and his

use specific quotes or facts and then respond

contributions to the English language. It's true: "He filled a universe with

words." Thanks to him and so many others, English now has over 500,000

words to choose from. I'm a little embarrassed that sometimes I can't

personal commentary

think of the right word to express myself! It's also amazing to read the

lists of words that we have borrowed from other languages. Some words I

always considered "American" are really derivatives from foreign languages.

Also, each generation adds its own unique words to our growing vocabulary;

I wonder what our linguistic legacy will be?

4. The Critical Analysis of Literature
In literature classes, you will be called upon to analyze poetry, plays, short stories, and novels. A critical or literary analysis requires that you go beyond the summary of a book report or the judgment required of a book review. A critical analysis involves a close reading of the text(s) and a thought-provoking assertion about one or more of the seven elements of fiction: plot, characters, setting, theme, symbolism, narrative voice, or writing style. Many literary analysis assignments will require secondary sources (outside research) to support your critique of the primary source (the text being examined).

See page 46 for an example of a literary analysis of a novel using outside sources and MLA documentation style.

5. The Bibliographic Essay

In classes that depend upon extensive research, such as some history or literature courses, the bibliographic essay asks that you compile a critical survey of a variety of sources concerning a particular subject (e.g., texts about the Vietnam War; the history of the critical response to a particular play). These types of essays help follow trends of scholarship and are vital for teachers and students to keep abreast on recent dialogues and topics of interest in their field. The bibliographic essay must assess the usefulness of the sources; therefore, it is best to organize the essay according to subtopics or chronologically.

The following bibliographic essay was written for a literature course and offers a work-by-work chronological overview of twentieth-century critics on Alexander Pope and his works.

introduce book and author | In his text <u>The Early Career of Alexander Pope</u>, George Sherburn | begins with a text that focuses on Pope's childhood

critical response to text | has written what is generally considered the definitive biography of

Pope's life up until 1727. This does not offer criticism of Pope's works, but | what this book does and does not do

hopes to enhance future criticism by shedding light on Pope's childhood,

education, and other influences that helped shape the man who would

become one of the greatest satirists in the English language. Like many of

general first person (not "I") | Pope's biographers, Sherburne tries to change the general opinion of Pope so that (we) can be more open to his works. Although he never actually discusses

Pope at the peak of his career, Sherburne certainly illuminates it from afar

by helping us understand the circumstances out of which his controversial | final comment on text

segue with concept of personality | personality emerged.

Edith Sitwell, in <u>Alexander Pope</u>, presents Pope as a kind, | introduce second author and title

loveable man and not the character with a "deformed spirit and mind" as | direct quotation shows close reading

many turn-of-the-century critics had labeled him. Although she does not

fully explain the reasons behind each of his infamous quarrels with his

peers, she hopes to justify his character so we may see beyond the man and

properly appreciate the works. This is a sympathetic portrait of a

misunderstood genius.

6. The Annotated Bibliography

It is important that students learn to critically assess sources rather than just gather them. Therefore, an annotated bibliography is often assigned as a part of a larger research project. An annotated bibliography requires you to carefully consider sources—the overall argument, the presentation of materials, and sometimes the usefulness for a given assignment. In an annotated bibliography, you provide a listing of sources (usually used for an assigned research paper), including full source information with each entry and a brief summary of the source's main points or arguments. Some annotated bibliography assignments may ask for a concluding comment about the source's value in terms of that particular research project. Some are only supposed to be sentences long, while others may be one or two typed pages for each source.

*The following example is a portion from an **annotated bibliography** written for a class on the works of Shakespeare. The teacher asked for two paragraphs for each source: one summarizing the source and the other assessing the source.*

Beckman, Margaret Boerner. "The Figure of Rosalind in <u>As You Like It</u>." <u>Shakespeare Quarterly</u> 29 (1987): 44-51.

full citation in MLA format

basis of argument

Beckman's article is strongly rooted in textual evidence from which emerges a very powerful argument that "to know Rosalind is to know that opposites can be reconciled" (52). Beckman begins by briefly describing the critical views of Harold Jenkins and C.L. Barber, which argue for and against the reconciliation of opposites, respectively. From these critical views, Beckman diverges and states her purpose as demonstrating how "Shakespeare shows man's 'possible perfection' rather than his 'certain imperfection,' presenting that perfection as a reconciliation of opposites in which both members of the opposition are retained in the face of all temptation to choose one or the other" (46). Physically, verbally, and psychologically, Rosalind's character is extremely complex and the "male/ female coincidence" leads to her as a symbol of that natural union of opposites.

direct quotation to support opinion

presents author's general argument

direct quotation in proper MLA format

Because this is a textual critique and I agree with most of Beckman's argument, I found this article both accessible and helpful. However, in an attempt to cover Rosalind's entire character, as well as to

critique of source

review all of the opposites she embodies, the argument seems rushed and superficial at times. In the end, this analysis fails to satisfy the reader's thirst for supporting details because of its lack of depth.

7. The Grant Proposal

A **grant proposal** is a specific type of proposal (as discussed under *Discipline Section II: Writing in the Social Sciences*). Rather than merely asking for permission to either research a topic or conduct studies, however, a grant proposal is looking for the funding to proceed with a particular project. Grant proposals are common in the fine arts because obtaining public or private funding can play a big part in seeing your artistic vision become a reality. Therefore, a grant proposal must be highly persuasive, professional, and thorough.

Find the right audience because your grant proposal is probably unsolicited (you are making the first move); therefore, you must send it to the appropriate people. Do your homework and make sure that your grant proposal is sent to a foundation or corporation that is somehow linked to your topic, medium, location, or subject. There should be a natural connection between your project and the organization that may sponsor it.

Package the grant proposal creatively, attractively, yet professionally. The appearance of your proposal must not only be letter perfect, but reflect the skills and creativity of its writers. This, in turn, mirrors the talent behind the final project at the heart of the proposal.

The format of a grant proposal is very straightforward, and you do not want to deviate from this very much as your readers come to expect serious grant proposals to look a certain way. For more details on writing grant proposals, an excellent source is The Foundation Center's Guide to Proposal Writing, eds. Jane C. Geever and Patricia McNeill.

Outline for a Grant Proposal:

All examples shown in this section were written by a non-profit organization, Collaborative Effect, which is comprised of artists who seek funding to establish an inner-city art programs for youths.

Cover letter
The **cover letter** should follow the format of a professional business letter (see The Letter under *Section IV: Writing in Business*). Be very specific: use a specific

salutation (do your homework and get a name!); make your request (the monetary amount you are looking for); explain why you are applying to this particular foundation; note any references to prior meetings or conversations (but avoid name dropping); describe the contents of the proposal package; explain the basics of the project, and offer to set up a meeting and/or to provide additional information.

Title page

Personalize this page by listing the name of the foundation to which you are applying. Choose your **title** carefully—don't try to be too cute, don't use common or familiar names that could be confusing. Instead, your title should be meaningful in some way. Because the proposal for Collaborative Effect is an artistic undertaking, the writers included a cover page before the title page, which consisted of their own original artwork that represents the theme of their mission.

Sample title page:

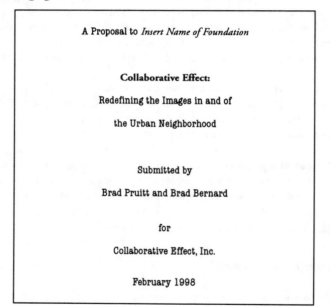

A Proposal to *Insert Name of Foundation*

Collaborative Effect:

Redefining the Images in and of

the Urban Neighborhood

Submitted by

Brad Pruitt and Brad Bernard

for

Collaborative Effect, Inc.

February 1998

Table of Contents

The **table of contents** should provide specific page numbers where the reader can find the major sections of the proposal. Do not include the cover letter, the title page, or the contents page in this listing.

Executive Summary

An **executive summary** should include one or two paragraphs that state the problem at hand. The next paragraph or two offers the solution you are proposing (a description of the project—who benefits from it, how and where it will operate, who will staff it). Follow this with one paragraph of the funding requirements, both the amount you are currently seeking and how you intend to obtain future funding. In the final paragraph, provide the name, history, purpose, and some of the activities of your organization. Although the executive summary includes these four very specific sections, write them in paragraph form without any divisions or headings. It should look more like an expository essay.

There is a direct relationship between the volume and depth of negative community images and the ability of central city residents to think positively about their long-term opportunities. Collaborative Effect recognizes that an effective method to promote substantial and sustainable community development is through the planning and the implementation of creative projects that have a major impact on the ability of central city youths to define themselves as healthy and vital members of our community.

statement of general problem

Collaborative Effect has developed an innovative and fresh approach based on the use of arts and the development of artists. This approach includes education, youth mentoring, and image creation/recreation. This philosophy has and will continue to have a major impact on the lives of central city residents by challenging and changing current perceptions of urban life. In addition, Collaborative Effect has developed a service approach for existing and emerging artists. The services use tested economic development principles as a basis for reaching this under-served entrepreneurial community. Through these various avenues, Collaborative Effect intends to redefine the images of central city life.

solution to the problem

The anticipated budget is $221,200 per year. Collaborative Effect is looking for $131,800 of that to be through grants. Income will come from mural productions, video productions, and art shows. Artists' Memberships fees will provide an additional annual income.

funding requirements

Collaborative Effect is a distinct and tax exempt entity located in the
central city of Milwaukee, Wisconsin, whose primary mission is redefining
the images in and of the urban neighborhood. It is staffed by volunteer
local artists, artisans, and musicians, who are aided by volunteers from
the business and academic communities. The organization's fundamental
principle is that a healthy neighborhood is comprised of many things
including positive images, creative outlets for residents, and economic
opportunities.

history of organization

Statement of Need

This section provides evidence supporting your assertion that there is a need for
this project. Use authorities in your field along with your own experience. Be
succinct yet persuasive in a logical statement that shows you understand and can
address the problem at hand.

Milwaukee's central city needs positive imagery and outlets for its
youth. Having been raised in Milwaukee's central city, and then working in
the middle and high schools there, the founders of Collaborative Effect
know first-hand the plight of this city. The depth and degree of negative
images reaching Milwaukee's African-American community, in addition to
the lack of resources, are root causes holding Milwaukee's central city
community in the grip of stark impoverishment and despair. Far too often,
the images and realities portrayed by the popular press are ones of violence,
neglect, and apathy. This type of portrayal fuels further violence, neglect,
and apathy. It is a cycle that perpetuates high crime rates, high unemployment
rates, and few new businesses being built by members of the African-
American community. As a result, young people growing up in Milwaukee's
central city do not see people actively involved in building neighborhoods;
they do not see people voting, and they do not see people impacting their own
daily lives. These images and realities need to change. Before developing
this proposal, Collaborative Effect undertook a year-long planning process
to access the best approach to redefine urban neighborhood images and

understand the problem at hand

field experience that led to proposal

assist existing and emerging artists in this community. The specifics of this
proposal are based on this assessment.

Program/Project Description

The **program description** offers the details alluded to in the Executive
Summary. It can include the background material and assessment of the
situation, specific explanations of aspects of the project that have already been
completed, are in the process of being completed, or are still in the planning
stages. The amount of information provided in this section is usually dependent
upon how long the organization has been providing services. If the descriptions
are theoretical only, this section is a bit shorter than if the organization has
successfully proven it can administer these programs.

Budget

When preparing the **budget**, keep these three simple rules in mind: be clear, be
honest, and be thorough. Foundations want to know exactly where the money
will go. Do your homework because if you receive the funding, you must
comply to the operating budget provided here.

Organization Information

Now that you have convinced your reader there is a problem and you have
formulated a working solution, take the time to **introduce you and your
organization** so that the foundation knows you are the best people to
implement this solution. Explain who you are, where you are located, how long
you have been working together, and any successful projects with which you
have already been involved.

Conclusion

In one or two paragraphs, **call attention to the future:** how your project will
positively affect the lives of its participants. If appropriate, outline follow-up
activities that may be undertaken (it prepares the foundation for your future
requests!). Make your final appeal for your project and your need for funding.
Don't be afraid to use a little emotion to make your case.

It is difficult to measure perception and image. To address this issue,

Collaborative Effect is interested in researching historical media coverage

and advertising. The conclusion of this study should result in a landmark

review of Milwaukee's image of its central city. For now, however,

Collaborative Effect can only look to the future. And with your foundation's

help, we can change the way the central city youths view their community by building their own niche within it. Together, we will create a healthy

and vibrant community that is economically sound, socially tolerant,

intellectually stimulating, and racially integrated through new and positive

images fostered by community education and services to artists.

Appendices (if applicable).
Not every proposal requires an **appendix**. It is a reference source for your readers that includes any information not presented elsewhere in the proposal, but that may be pertinent for your request. Some items found in an appendix could include a list of the Board of Directors, selected press clippings, an annual report, an IRS tax exemption letter, audited financial statements, and a list of major contributors.

WD
Box
7

"Don'ts" for Grant Proposals

✓ Don't use sloppy numbers in your budget.

✓ Don't exaggerate your experience or expectations.

✓ Don't get too personal.

✓ Don't be a victim of poor or incomplete research.

✓ Don't use tiny print or bind your final proposal.

✓ Don't be vague or allusive.

✐ DOCUMENTATION IN THE HUMANITIES

When writing papers in a humanities course, it is your responsibility to clarify the guidelines of any given assignment. This includes things such as length of assignment, research requirements and/or restrictions, and documentation style.

The two standard documentation styles for most humanities courses are the *Modern Language Association* (MLA) format and *The Chicago Manual of Style* (CMS or CM) format.

Modern Language Association Sample Paper

The concept behind the MLA format is simple: As the writer, you must clearly indicate all quotations, paraphrases, and summaries taken from outside sources each time they appear in your paper and then, on a separate page at the end of your paper, provide the complete bibliographic information of each source used.

You indicate borrowed materials within your paper (in-text or internal citations) with a combination of signal or introductory phrases before the borrowed material and a parenthetical indicator following it. Your reader could then match this information with the full source listing provided alphabetically on the "Works Cited" page.

Either in the signal phrase (occurs before the borrowed material) or in the parenthetical indicator (occurs after the borrowed material), the author and/or text is noted along with a specific page number of where the material could be found in the original source.

> The economic and political conditions that contributed to the rise of
>
> Communism and Pre-World War II Germany still exist today, including
>
> "economic dislocation, xenophobia and populism" (Binyan 19). *[Last name*
>
> *and page number of source in parenthetical indicator]*

> Journalist Liu Binyan asserts, "The Soviet Union and Nazi Germany may no
>
> longer exist, but the economic, social and political factors that led to their
>
> emergence still do—economic dislocation, xenophobia and populism" (19).
>
> *[Name provided in signal phrase, so page number only in parenthetical*
>
> *indicator]*

Smith 8

Works Cited

Binya, Liu, "Civilization Grafting." <u>Writing in the Disciplines: A Reader</u>
<u>for Writers</u>. Eds. Mary Lynch Kennedy, William J. Kennedy, and Hadley M.
Smith. New Jersey: Prentice-Hall, Inc., 1996.

⌨ **For online help with MLA documentation, visit**
<u>www.english.uiuc.edu/cws/wworkshop/bibliostyles</u>
or
<u>www.lib.usm.edu/~instruct/guides/ugindex</u>

MODERN LANGUAGE ASSOCIATION SAMPLE PAPER

For an introductory literature course, Edward Johnson, a first-year student, wrote the following literary analysis of The Great Gatsby *and "Winter Dreams" using MLA internal citations and a works cited page. The assignment asked for a four-to-five page typed research paper on F. Scott Fitzgerald and at least one of his works.*

This is a typical **open-ended assignment**, *meaning the students had to find their own topic within the broader subject given.*

Edward H. Johnson

Professor Manion

English 001

6 November 1999

double-space heading

Johnson 1 | running header

Reinventing Oneself:

center title, do not bold or underline

F. Scott Fitzgerald's Road to The Great Gatsby

underline or italicize titles of novels

The Great Gatsby is often considered the quintessential novel of the

American Dream. It is a timeless story of romance, illusion, money, and

status—themes all deeply felt by its author, F. Scott Fitzgerald. These

elements are explored in nearly all of Fitzgerald's works. In discussing the

autobiographical nature of his fiction, Fitzgerald once said, "The whole idea

of Gatsby is the unfairness of a poor young man not being able to marry a

girl with money. The theme comes up again and again because I lived it"

citation with author and page number

put titles of short stories in quotation marks

(Turnbull 150). The concept of striving for the unobtainable, whether in life

or love, also appears in the short story "Winter Dreams." This short story is

one of a group of stories written by Fitzgerald wherein he explores concepts

later incorporated into The Great Gatsby. The theme of reinventing oneself,

driven by poor perceptions of parents and background, while seeking the

trappings and embodiment of success, were lived by Fitzgerald, developed

in "Winter Dreams," and fully realized in The Great Gatsby.

three point thesis statement

Fitzgerald's lifelong self-conscious feeling of social inferiority, bred primarily by his utter disapproval of his parents, drove him to rise above his background and become a celebrated author. Intensely goal-oriented, he dreamed of being a success, but always felt hamstrung by his family background. Fitzgerald describes his St. Paul childhood home as, "A house below the average on a street above the average" (Eble 19). Fitzgerald's father was depicted as a man who could not hold a job—an abject failure.

no use of "I" or "we" throughout the paper

His mother's immigrant family, although somewhat wealthy, was "straight potato-famine Irish" (Eble 20). Her father earned his money in the wholesale grocery business. Between his parents, thought, it was his eccentric, extravagant mother for whom Fitzgerald reserved most of his scorn. He felt she constantly humiliated him. Scott Donaldson, summarizing Fitzgerald's frustrations and desires, notes, "From her (his mother) he inherited his compulsive drive for social success; from her he inherited 'black Irish' roots that hardly facilitated success. He had to make it on his own, through his own accomplishments" (15). This sense of turmoil motivated Fitzgerald to seek social acceptance through popularity.

page # only because author's name was in sentence

The craving for social acceptance consumed young Fitzgerald, and instilled in him the desire to reinvent himself. At an early age Fitzgerald wrote, directed, and starred in theatrical productions. He enrolled at Princeton, a long way socially and geographically from St. Paul. There he fancied himself as the star of the college football team, but he was cut from the squad shortly after practices began. While at Princeton, Fitzgerald sought, and lost, the presidency of the Triangle Club. His academic career soured. Donaldson describes Fitzgerald's relationship with Princeton accordingly: "He courted Princeton's approval, ardently and unsuccessfully" (18). Ironically, it will be these social frustrations encountered in his early

"acceptance" serves as transition between paragraphs

youth and at Princeton that supply a large measure of the recipe Fitzgerald
used to create a triumphant literary reputation.

From early on, Fitzgerald knew he wanted to be a successful writer.
Shortly after his time in college, Fitzgerald wrote to his friend, the writer
Edmund Wilson, "I want to be one of the greatest writers who have ever
lived, don't you?" (Eble 30). Matthew Bruccoli, author of <u>Some Sort of
Epic Grandeur</u>, indicates this desire was in part due to "Scott's drive for
recognition [which] required an audience and admiring companions" (26).

student
adds words
[   ] to
make the
sentence
flow

Starting at a young age, Fitzgerald worked very had to refine his craft,
and his early success was deemed "a triumph of will" (Eble 67). It is in the
achievement of <u>Gatsby</u> that "Fitzgerald's deepest feelings about his status,
his desires, his hunger for love and for worldly success are . . . set forth"
(Eble 105). In preparing to write <u>The Great Gatsby</u>, Fitzgerald experimented
in several short stories with different themes that later appear in the
classic novel. The tale of Dexter Green in "Winter Dreams," a story that
closely prefigures <u>Gatsby</u>, has many parallels to the life of Fitzgerald.

. . . indicates
three or
more words
have been
removed
from the
direct
quotation

Much of the discussion of the autobiographical content of "Winter
Dreams" (and <u>Gatsby</u>) relates to the similarities between Fitzgerald's and
Dexter's illusions and desires for wealth as embodied by the pursuit of an
ultimately unobtainable rich girl by a poor boy. There is another
resemblance, however, and that is the common themes of parental
embarrassment and perceptions of inferior social standing spurring the
characters to reinvent themselves. Dexter, like Fitzgerald, comes from a
middle-class upbringing. Similar to Fitzgerald's grandfather, Dexter's father
is in the grocery business. However, instead of a wealthy wholesaler,
Dexter's parent is a single-store retailer. Dexter, like Fitzgerald, works to
separate himself from his world and enter the moneyed society. Not content

WD indicates "Winter Dreams" merely with association with "glittering things," Dexter feels the need to possess them (WD 221). Symbolic of his attempt to hold a "glittering thing," Dexter perceives he must surmount, namely, his parental background and geographic inferiority on his route to realizing his "winter dreams."

One of the impediments to true societal acceptance Dexter feels he must overcome is his mother. She is described as "a Bohemian of the peasant class . . . [who] talked broken English to the end of her days" (WD 225). Dexter also harbors sensitivity to where he lives. He caddies at an exclusive golf resort, and lives in the nearby Black Bear Village. Yet when asked his hometown, he names Keeble, 30 miles away from his birthplace, as his residence. To Dexter, "Country towns were well enough to come from if they weren't inconveniently in sight and used as footstools by fashionable lakes" (WD 225). In Dexter's mind, whether one caddies for the rich, or lives in a town next to their playground, in order to enjoy the privileges of wealth, one must have separation between oneself and this background.

the student doesn't end a paragraph with a quotation, but evaluates it

Dexter eventually gains separation from his hometown, and his family, by moving to New York to run his thriving business. This separation is so successful that a business associate remarks, "That's funny—I thought men like you were probably born and raised on Wall Street" (WD 234). Even though financially successful, Dexter still feels restrained by his upbringing. The symbol the freedom enjoyed by the privileged upper class is the much-desired butterfly, Judy Jones. As related by Robert and Helen Roulston in The Winding Road to West Egg, "Thus she (Judy Jones) epitomizes an insouciant power ever unattainable for Dexter as the son of a Bohemian woman and of the proprietor of the second-best grocery store in a resort town" (121). Fitzgerald's preoccupations with family and surroundings as a bar to

the student adds (Judy Jones) to clarify "she"

high society, explored in "Winter Dreams" are more fully developed in The
Great Gatsby.

The story of James Gatz (Jay Gatsby) is one of reinvention, replacing
one family history with a completely new one. A large part of Gatsby deals
with the acquisition of wealth as a means to capture the rich society girl who
is otherwise unobtainable. Interestingly, though, Gatsby begins his journey of
reinvention at a point many years before he meets Daisy Fay—the object of
his affection. James Gatz is born the son of "shiftless and unsuccessful farm
people" from North Dakota (GG 104). They are "Unimaginative, impoverished
German farmers" (Ornstein 57). Susan Resneck Parr declares, "To some
extent, Gatsby transforms himself from Jimmy Gatz to Jay Gatsby because
he was unhappy with his parents: In his imagination, he 'had never really
accepted them as his parents at all' (GG 118)" (63). Once again, Fitzgerald's
background serving as a source for his fiction can by seen clearly. Like

Critic Parr cites Great Gatsby and the student then cites Parr

Fitzgerald, Gatsby attempts to separate himself from his parent's inadequate,
immigrant, Midwestern background, and is drawn toward a "future glory"
(GG 105). Similarly, Gatsby feels himself an outsider. He never seems
completely comfortable with the transition from Jimmy Gatz. According to
John Callahan, "Sensitive to the demarcations of background, money, and
status, Gatsby knew he was in Daisy's house by a colossal accident.
However glorious might be his future as Jay Gatsby, he was at present a
penniless young man without a past, and at any moment the invisible cloak
of his uniform might slip from his shoulders" (17). The sensitivity to
geographic background is further described by the passage, "Contending on
that ground, Gatsby may well pay an emotional tithe to the poor boy from
North Dakota, and again feel he has no right to touch Daisy's hand"
(Callahan 22). There is a sense Gatsby feels himself an imposter. Gatsby

GG distinguishes this quote from those taken from "Winter Dreams"

worries about how Nick perceives him, remarking, "I didn't want you to think I was just some nobody" (GG 71). Although never completely satisfied, Gatsby's reinvention of himself, largely due to his dissatisfaction with his parents and his youthful environment, mirrors Fitzgerald's.

The Great Gatsby and the writings of F. Scott Fitzgerald have been studied extensively, and Fitzgerald acknowledged his works and characters were largely autobiographical. Gatsby is a multi-faceted book by a brilliant writer who explores many complex themes that have resonated with readers since its publication. One of those themes is Fitzgerald's insecurity in a social hierarchy based on birth-right and wealth. Attributable somewhat to his perceptions of failed parents and poor background, this autobiographical theme drove him to reinvent himself both in and through his literature, particularly in the familiar characters of Dexter Green and Jay Gatsby.

restatement
of thesis

`running header`

`centered`
`do not bold`
Works Cited `do not underline`

`hanging indent`

Bruccoli, Matthew J. <u>Some Sort of Epic Grandeur</u>. New York:

Harcourt Brace Jovanovich, 1981. `period after every entry`

Callahan, John F. "F. Scott Fitzgerald's Evolving American Dream: `article from a scholarly journal`

`double-space entire page`
The 'Pursuit of Happiness' in Gatsby, Tender is the Night, and The

Last Tycoon." <u>Twentieth Century Literature</u> 42 (1996): 51 pars. 38

Oct. 1999 http://proquest.umi.com.

`entries listed` Donaldson, Scott. <u>Fool For Love</u>. New York: Congdon & Weed,
`alphabetically by last name` Inc., 1983.

Eble, Kenneth. <u>F. Scott Fitzgerald</u>. New York: Twayne Publishers, 1963.

`reprinted book` Fitzgerald, F. Scott. <u>The Great Gatsby</u>. 1925. New York: Scribner Paperback

Fiction, 1995.

`same author as previous entry` ---. "Winter Dreams." The Short Stories of F. Scott Fitzgerald. Ed. Matthew

`two primary sources`

J. Bruccoli. New York: Charles Scribner's Sons, 1989. 217-236.

Ornstein, Robert. "Scott Fitzgerald's Fable of East and West." <u>Twentieth</u>

<u>Century Interpretations of The Great Gatsby</u>. Ed. Ernest Lockridge.

Englewood Cliffs: Prentice-Hall, Inc. 1968. 54-60.

`article from a collection` Parr, Susan Resneck. "The Idea of Order at West Egg." <u>New Essays on The</u>

<u>Great Gatsby</u>. Ed. Matthew J. Bruccoli. Cambridge: Cambridge

University Press, 1985. 59-78.

Roulston, Robert and Helen H. Roulston. <u>The Winding Road to West Egg</u>.

Lewisburg: Bucknell University Press, 1995.

Turnbull, Andrew. <u>Scott Fitzgerald</u>. New York: Charles Scribner's, 1962.

Chicago Manual of Style Sample Paper

The concept behind the CMS format is simple: As the writer, you must give the full bibliographic information in the form of endnotes or footnotes of any quotations, paraphrases, and summaries each time you use any materials from each outside source. Footnotes appear at the bottom of the page containing the relevant citation, and endnotes appear in a sequential listing on a separate page labeled *Notes* following the final page of text.

Example of CMS endnotes:

During the 1920s and 30s, women who lived under some authoritarian regimes were offered new legal rights. In most of these states, however, there was a "counterbalancing reassertion of older values, notable an emphasis on home life and motherhood."[1]

15

NOTES

[1]Anthony Esler, <u>The Western World: Prehistory to the Present</u>, (New Jersey: Prentice-Hall, Inc.), 1994: 939.

If additional borrowed material is used from the same source later in the paper, another footnote or endnote is used each time the source is mentioned, but with less bibliographic information.

[2]Esler, <u>Western</u>, 948.

If your second reference from the **same source** appears in the text immediately following the first reference and full citation, use the word *Ibid.* (short for ibidem, meaning "in the same place") followed by the page number.

Example of CMS footnotes with subsequent citations from same source:

Between the two wars, what has been termed "the modern notion of womanhood"[1] evolved in many countries. Yet under Fascist governments, "glorifying male strength, virility, and force assigned women a secondary role in society."[2]

[1]Anthony Esler, <u>The Western World: Prehistory to the Present</u>, (New Jersey: Prentice-Hall, Inc.) 1994: 938.

[2]Ibid., 939.

For CMS papers, footnotes and endnotes can also include additional information that the reader should be aware of, but to include it within the text of the paper would be disruptive to the flow of the narrative. These **informational notes** are cited and documented exactly like the source notes.

A separate listing of all the sources (a **bibliography**) can be required for longer research papers. A **bibliography** may be organized alphabetically by authors' last names. For papers that include many sources, the bibliography is first organized by categories (with headings) and then alphabetized within each category. Typical categories include: Primary Sources, Secondary Sources, Books, Journal Articles, Unpublished Documents, and Electronic Sources.

Each entry in the bibliography is single-spaced; double-space only between entries. Use a hanging indent (only the first line of the entry is left-flush).

It is important to remember that the **CMS is not a handbook for academic writing**. It is a stylebook for professional publishers. Therefore, it does not have hard-set rules on things such as title pages and citation styles, but offers stylistic options instead.

The following paper uses CMS as interpreted by Kate L. Turabian's <u>A Manual for Writers</u>.

⌨ **For online help with CMS documentation, visit**
www.wisc.edu/writing/Handbook

⌨ **For online help with Turabian documentation, visit**
www.lib.usm.edu/~instruct/guides/ugindex

The following pages are taken from a research paper written by Michael O'Malley, a fourth-year history major, on the critical debate surrounding The Great Irish Famine. It uses endnotes for documentation of sources following the Chicago Manual of Style. It also incorporates informational endnotes. The teacher did require both a separate title page and a bibliography.

THE GREAT IRISH FAMINE, 1845-1850:

An Historiographical Essay

by

Michael O'Malley

History 395

Dr. Janet Nolan

May 1996

The objective of this paper is to provide a record of the historical debate on the Great Irish Famine of 1845-1850. Historians of the Famine agree that almost every harvest of potatoes, the subsistence food for most of Ireland's inhabitants before the Famine, failed totally or partially between 1845 and 1850. These writers also agree that the potato crops' destruction resulted in starvation and death throughout Ireland. However, the historians disagree on several issues. One of the most contentious issues is whether or not the Famine was a central event or watershed in nineteenth-century Irish history. Several questions are related to this issue including: What was the number of excess deaths during the Famine? What role did the Famine play in the decline of Gaelic society and culture? Was the Famine a central event in Irish emigration history? Historians also differ on the issue of whether the British government was responsible for suffering during the Famine. Nationalist historians such as John Mitchel entered the debate immediately after the Famine claiming that it was a watershed in Irish history. They argued that it led to more than a million deaths and the British government caused most of the suffering.[1] More recently, revisionist historians such as Roy Foster have taken the opposite view claiming that the Famine was not a central event in Irish history. They assert instead that less than one million people died and that Gaelic society was already changing before the late 1840s. Revisionists also downplay the negative role of the British government during the Famine.[2] The conclusions drawn by the nationalists and revisionists have recently been reexamined by post-revisionist historians of the famine such as Cormac O'Grada and Robert Cally. These writers argue convincingly that the Famine was a watershed in Irish history. They prove that the Famine played a significant role in the destruction of Ireland's traditional culture. They also argue that it had a catastrophic

clearly state purpose of paper

refers reader to endnote #1

refers reader to endnote #2

page # for first page differs from others

1

human impact and that is was a watershed in Irish emigration history. In
addition, they show that the government's failure to relieve hunger was
responsible for starvation during the Faminine.[3]

Nationalist authors such as John Mitchel claimed that the Famine was
a central event in Irish history. According to Mitchel, one and a half million
people died in the Famine. Millions more were left landless and homeless.
Mitchel argued that the British government caused this suffering. In his
view, Britain's policies during the Famine were genocidal both in intent and
result. For example, he asserted that the government passed legislation to
clear the land of Irish farmers and cottiers. Having made these people
homeless, the government then banished them from the country by
emigration. According to Mitchel, the government's genocidal policies
resulted in mass starvation and exodus⊙

cite all borrowed material, not just direct quotations

Cecil Woodham-Smith sympathized with the nationalist interpretation
of the Famine. Like Mitchel, she argued that the disaster was a central event
in Irish social history. She supported her argument by examining the
demographic toll of the Famine. She calculated that the disaster killed over a
million people and estimated that another one and a half million fled Famine-
stricken Ireland and travelled to North America, England, and Wales. The
author showed that excess mortality and emigration caused depopulation
throughout Ireland. Leinster lost over fifteen percent of its population, Ulster
sixteen percent, Muster twenty-three percent, and Connaught twenty-eight
percent. According to the author, this depopulation changed the Irish
countryside. Between 1845 and 1851, for example, nearly 360,000 mud
huts and half of all small holdings under five acres disappeared.[5]

statistics are stated not quoted

consecutive
numbering
of pages

NOTES

centered
all caps
do not bold or underline

indent
and label
each note

[1]The nationalist view is supported as early as John Mitchel's 1861 study <u>The Last Conquest of Ireland (Perhaps)</u>. Cecil Woodham-Smith also sympathizes with the nationalist interpretation of the famine.

use a period after each entry

[2]This view is defended in Steven Ellis's "Nationalist Historiography and the English and Gaelic Worlds in the Late Middle Ages," in <u>Interpreting Irish History: The Debate on Historical Revisionism, 1938-1994</u>, ed. Ciaran Brady (Blackrock, Co. Dublin: Irish Academic Press, 1994), 161-180.

informational note cited same as source note

double-
space
between
entries

[3]Irish historians Margaret E. Crawford, Mary Daly, David Dickerson, and Cormac Ó'Gráda support this interpretation.

single-
space
entry

[4]James Donnelly, "The Great Famine: Its Interpreters, Old and New," <u>History Ireland</u> 1:3 (1993): 30-31.

[5]Ibid., 411-412.

note #5 comes from the same source as note #4

consecutive
page
numbering

list entries
alpabetically
by authors'
last names

hanging
indent

5
space
indent for
subsequent
lines

BIBLIOGRAPHY | centered
all caps
do not bold or underline

Bradshaw, Brendan. "Nationalism and Historical Scholarship in Modern
Ireland." Irish Historical Studies 26 (1988-9): 329-51. | single-space
each entry

use a period
after each entry

Crawford, Margaret E. "Food and Famine," in The Great Irish Famine, ed.
Cathal Póirtéir. Dublin: Mercier Press, 1995, 60-73.

Daly, Mary. "The Operations of Famine Relief, 1845-47," in Ibid., 174-184.

Donnelly, James. "The Great Famine: Its Interpreters, Old and New," History
Ireland 1:3 (1993): 30-31.

double-space
between entries

Ellis, Steven. "Nationalist Historiography and the English and Gaelic Worlds
in the Late Middle Ages" in Interpreting Irish History: The Debate on
Historical Revisionism, 1938-1994, ed. Ciaran Brady. Blackrock, Co.
Dublin: Irish Academic Press, 1994, 161-180.

Fitzpatrick, David, "Flight From Famine," in Oceans of Consolation: Personal
Accounts of Irish Migration to Australia. Ithaca, New York: Cornell
University Press, 1994.

Geary, Laurence M. "Famine, Fever, and the Bloody Flux," in The Great Irish
Famine, 74-85.

Kinealy, Christine. "The Role of the Poor Law during the Famine" in The
Great Calamity: The Irish Famine, 1845-52. Dublin: Gill and
Macmillan, 1994, 104-122.

Miller, Kerby. Emigrants and Exiles: Ireland and the Irish Exodus to North
America. New York: Oxford University Press, 1985.

Smith, Cecil Woodham. The Great Hunger: Ireland, 1845-1849. London:
Hamish Hamilton, 1962.

The following page is taken from a first-year student's research paper in a religious studies course. It uses footnotes and slightly different rules for pagination as required by the teacher. A separate title page or a bibliography was not required for this assignment.

| running header

Cathy Morrell

Religious Studies 101 } heading as required by teacher

Dr. Joyce

14 November 1987

The Impact on Magic on Early Christian Society | centered, do not bold, do not underline

5 space indent → John Aseldon asserted, "The Reason of a Thing is not to be inquired after, til you are sure the Thing itself be so. We commonly are at What's the Reason for It? before we are sure of the Thing."1 Any study of magic immediately runs into problems for want of the concrete definition demanded by Seldon. How can we be sure of the Thing to be studied when it is constantly changing to accommodate social pressures of each age? | no extra spacing between paragraphs

Definitions can sometimes be determined by looking at function. According to Marwick, magic has been used to:

4 spaces → Provide necessary outlets for repressed hostility, frustrations and anxiety; serve as media through which real or imagined episodes dramatize and reinforce social norms, in that
4 space block indent → antisocial or socially inadequate conduct is attributed, sometimes either to the accused or to his believed victim; . . . reflect the incidence of tension between the accuser and the magician.2

| single-space long quotes

no quotation marks needed

During the time of the Early Christian Church, magic needed no concrete definition. "Magic was viewed as real and efficacious . . . the people of this age knew magic when they saw it."3

_____

single-space each entry | 1Geertz, Hildred, <u>Journal of Interdisciplinary History</u> V: 1 (Summer 1995): 71–89.

| double-space between entries

2Marwick, M.G. <u>Articles of Witchcraft, Magic and Demonology</u> (1992): 231.

3Francis, James, "Apollonius of Tyana" Subversive Virtue: Asceticism and Authority in the 2nd Century Pagan World (1995): 92. use a period after each entry

Discipline Section II: Writing in the Social Sciences

The social sciences encompass a variety of subjects, including anthropology, communications, criminal justice, economics, education, political science, psychology, social work, and sociology (sometimes business is considered a social science, but in this supplement it is treated separately under *Discipline Section IV: Writing in Business*). The foundation of these subjects is defined as "the branch of learning concerned with using the process of scientific inquiry to study the structure of society and the activity of its members, including human behavior, relationships, social conditions, conduct, and customs." The social sciences concentrate on the basic systems and processes that together form our social and cultural environment; therefore, writing in the social sciences presents findings based on factual research and interpretations based on logic, reason, and evidence.

RESEARCH SOURCES

Library research is an integral part of the writing projects required in most of these subjects, yet researchers often engage in fieldwork as well. Social scientists rely on scholarly books and articles, but also on statistical research, government documents, and newspaper articles. As part of the fieldwork, they often engage in interviews, surveys, polls, and observations in order to collect quantifiable data to support the hypothesis, or educated guess, which they are hoping to prove.

There are quite a few sources of general information for the social sciences to begin your research. For more specific reference sources, see the appropriate subject category provided here.

Titles followed by an asterisk (*) indicate that the source also comes in some sort of electronic format (website, CD-ROM, online database, etc.). Always check with your librarian to see what is available to you.

General Social Science Research Sources

African American Encyclopedia
American Statistics Index (ASI)*
Bibliografia Chicano: A Guide to
   Information Sources
CQ Researcher*
Dictionary of Mexican American History
Encyclopedia of Black America
Handbook of North American Indians
Harvard Encyclopedia of American
   Ethnic Groups
Human Resources Abstracts*
Index to International Statistics (IIS)*

International Encyclopedia of the
   Social Sciences
PAIS (Public Affairs Information Service)*
Population Index*
Reference Encyclopedia of the American Indian
Reference Library of Black America
Social Sciences Citation Index*
Social Sciences Index*
Statistical Reference Index (SRI)*
Women's Studies: A Guide to Information
   Sources

Government Documents

Government documents can provide vital information to social scientists because they usually contain complete, accurate, and up-to-date facts and figures on a variety of topics.

Monthly Catalog of the United States
   Government Publications
The Congressional Information Service Index

The American Statistics Index
Index to U.S. Government Periodicals

Newspaper Sources

New York Times Index
Newsbank
Lexis/Nexis
InfoTrac's National Newspaper Index

Databases

Cendata
PsycINFO
ERIC
Social Scisearch
Information Science Abstracts

Economic Literature Index
ABI/INFORM
Legal Resource Index
Managmeent Contents
PTST + S Indexes

*Check with your librarian to see what databases are available to you.

Anthropology

Abstracts in Anthropology
Anthropological Literature*

Anthropological Index*
Dictionary of Anthropology
Encyclopedia of Cultural Anthropology

Criminal Justice

*Criminology, Penology, and Police
Science Abstracts*
Criminal Justice Abstracts*
Criminal Justice Periodicals Index*

Dictionary of Crime
Encyclopedia of Crime and Justice
Encyclopedia of World Crime
Index to Legal Periodicals*

Education

Critical Dictionary of Educational Concepts
Current Index to Journals in Education*
Dictionary of Education
Education Index*

Encyclopedia of Educational Research
Facts on File*
Resources in Education*

Economics

Dictionary of Economics
The Encyclopedia of Banking and Finance
Journal of Economic Literature
The McGraw-Hill Dictionary of Modern Economics
The Wall Street Journal Index

Political Science

ABC Political Science*
American Political Dictionary
*CIS Index to Publications of the
United States Congress*
*CRIS: The Combined Retrospective Index
Setto Journals in Political Science,
1886–1974*
Dictionary of Modern Politics
Dictionary of Political Ideologies
Encyclopedia of Modern World Politics
Encyclopedia of the Third World

*Encyclopedia of the United Nations and
International Agreements*
Europa World Year Book
Foreign Affairs Bibliography
*ISLA (Information Services on Latin
America)*
International Political Science Abstracts*
United States Political Science Documents
U.S. Serial Set Index*
Worldmark Encyclopedia of the Nations

Psychology

Author Index to Psychological Index and Psychological Abstracts
Biographical Dictionary of Psychology
Contemporary Psychology

Cumulative Subject Index to Psychological Abstracts
Encyclopedia of Psychology
International Encyclopedia of Psychiatry, Psychology, Psychoanalysis and Neurology
*Psychology Abstracts**

Sociology and Social Work

*Encyclopedia of Social Work**
Encyclopedia of Sociology
Poverty and Human Resources Abstracts
Rural Sociology Abstracts
*Sage Family Studies Abstracts**
Social Work Research and Abstracts
*Sociological Abstracts**

Non-Library Sources

Other important information in the social sciences may be obtained through interviews, surveys, questionnaires, polls, and site visits (observations). Be prepared to do the necessary legwork in order to obtain supporting evidence for your project.

Although the Internet can provide easy access to other universities and colleges around the world, there is also a lot of misinformation floating around out there. Ultimately, each teacher has the final word as to whether or not Internet sources are allowed for any given research assignment.

✐ WRITING EXPECTATIONS IN THE SOCIAL SCIENCES

Assignments for writing in the social sciences begin by asking questions or identifying problems related to particular phenomena. From this question, the student forms a hypothesis (an educated guess) based on certain assumptions that have been made. The student then tries to verify or prove the hypothesis by making a series of careful observations, assembling and analyzing data, and determining a clear pattern of response. In the end, the data must be compiled and the findings presented in a clear, coherent written manner.

The *language* of the social science paper tends to be more formal than that of the humanities paper, and uses more technical or field jargon. To explain tables and graphs, common statistical vocabulary is expected, but it is also important to convert the technical language into plain English in order to explain what all the data mean to your analysis.

Remember that the clearest writing in the social sciences comes from defining new or uncommon terms, concepts, or jargon. Try not to simply offer a textbook definition, but to explain through descriptions, analogies, and even classifications. It helps to provide clear, concrete examples of concepts and theories, including visual aids to present numeric data.

✍ ORGANIZATIONAL PATTERNS IN THE SOCIAL SCIENCES

The social sciences rely on many organizational patterns to present their findings depending on the context: chronological; narration; process; cause/effect; compare/contrast; description; analysis; classification; response; problem/solution, and question/answer. In fact, most social science papers overlap a number of these organizational patterns within one piece of writing.

Most writing in the social sciences has these distinct parts: introduction, discussion, and conclusion. Other common sections include background, methods and materials, and recommendations. What these are called and how they are formatted depends on the specific writing task.

✍ DOCUMENT DESIGN BASICS FOR THE SOCIAL SCIENCES

The general principles covered under **Document Design Basics** regarding margins and fonts should be followed for most of the writing done in courses in the social science discipline, but they also clarify your use of technical jargon and appropriateness of using first (I) or third person (they) in the paper.

The social science paper is usually divided into parts using appropriate internal headings. Each section is written as its own entity—with a beginning, a middle, and an end—so it makes sense both on its own and in context with the rest of the paper. The body of the paper may include tables, charts, graphs, or illustrations to present quantitative and numeric data.

Most classes within the social sciences follow the format and documentation style as presented in the *Publication Manual of the American Psychological Association,* 4th edition (referred to as APA style).

Title Page

For most social science papers, use a title page. Expectations occur because the APA manual has no set of guidelines for the title page. The information generally includes a full title, the student's name, course number and name, teacher's name, and the date. This is centered with ample spacing in the page layout (see example APA paper at the end of this section). On the title page and all subsequent pages, type a two or three word abbreviated title followed by the page number, flush right, approximately one-half inch from the top of the page.

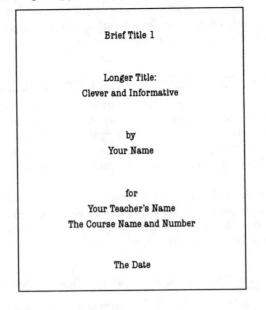

Abstract

An abstract is presented on a separate page, immediately following the title page. The heading of the page is *Abstract*—centered, first letter capitalized only. Double-space throughout the entire page. There are no paragraph indents used. The abstract provides a brief summary of the main point of your paper. See the sample social science paper at the end of this section for an example of an abstract.

Margins and Line Spacing

Follow the general **Document Design Basics** in this supplement. Double-space throughout the paper, and indent the first line of each paragraph one-half inch (about five spaces). For long quotations (longer than 40 words), indent each line one-half inch from the left margin. Continue to double-space preceding the quotation, within the quotation, and following the quotation. Quotation marks are not needed for longer quotes.

Visuals

For APA papers, visuals are either tables or figures (including charts, graphs, illustrations, maps, and photographs). Statistical and mathematical copy can also be presented in this way.

Tables are labeled with arabic numerals; do not add suffix letters or additional numbers to these (incorrect: Table 3b). Place the label left-flush above the table, with a brief, but informative, underlined title on the following line.

Any additional explanatory information appears immediately below the table, left-flush, doubled-spaced following the word _Note_. These may be written as complete sentences or clarifying phrases.

Example of APA table:

Table 12
Performance Scores of Students with Different College Majors

	History	Psychology	Physics	Philosophy
Language Test	87	82	78	85
Math Test	76	80	92	87
Science Test	45.9	67	88	73

Note. Student participants were all juniors and seniors currently on the Dean's list for at least two sequential semesters.

An informative table supplements (not duplicates) the text. In the text, refer to the tables by their numbers. "As shown in Table 12 . . . ," but do not refer to tables "above" or "below" the text or by page numbers.

If the table (or figure) is **taken from another source** and not compiled by the student from his or her own data, the bibliographical information appears in a note, and not on the References page at the end of the text. The following example includes suggested wording for using tables or figures from an APA journal. You must obtain the author's permission to use the table or figure and give APA full credit as copyright holder. (If submitting your article for publication, include the letter of permission with the final manuscript copy.)

Material taken from an article:

Note. From "Title of Article," by author's first name, last name, date, Journal in which Article Appeared, vol, p. #. Copyright date by the American Psychological Association (or Name of Appropriate Copyright Holder). Adapted (reprinted) with permission of the author.

Material taken from a book:

Note. From Title of Book (pg. #), by author's first name, last name, date, Place of Publication: Publisher. Copyright date by the Name of Copyright Holder. Adapted (reprinted) with permission of the author.

Figures are labeled by the word "Figure" (not abbreviated) and the consecutive arabic number followed by a period. Place the label below the figure and follow it with a caption. The **caption** is the explanation of the figure and serves as the title for the figure as well; therefore, it must be brief, yet informative.

Example of APA figure:

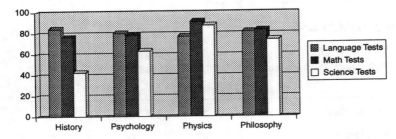

Figure 4. Double-spaced descriptive phrase or sentence that adds any needed information

to help clarify the figure.

A useful figure supplements (not duplicates) the text. The reader should not have to refer to the text to understand the figure. In the text, refer to the figures by their numbers. "As shown in Figure 4 . . ." Do not refer to tables "above" or "below" the text or by page numbers.

Statistics may be presented in either tables or figures. Do not give a reference for commonly known statistics. Do give a reference for (1) a less common statistic, such as one that has appeared in journals, but not handbooks (2) a controversial statistic, or (3) a statistic that is itself the focus of your paper.

All visuals should be discussed within the text of the paper, and the visuals should be placed as close to this discussion as possible.

✎ Assignments in the Social Sciences

1. The Experience Paper
   The experience paper (or observation paper) is a common social science assignment. In order to complete this type of writing, you will be asked to record your reactions and observations to some type of field trip or site visit. These assignments vary by subject. For example, a psychology student visits a private mental health clinic for a day, an education student sits in on a class that uses distance learning, a political science student observes a day in the life of a state representative, a sociology student meets with workers at a health facility on a reservation, or a criminology student

attends a trial. For such an assignment, do your homework before the visit so that you are prepared for what you might see. Observe rather than interact, and take good notes, perhaps (with permission) even using a small tape recorder to document your observations and reactions as they occur.

The following example is taken from an **experience paper** *written by Megan Rosichan, a junior political science major who was assigned to spend a day at a courthouse and record all that she observed.*

(I) visited the First District Court of Minnesota on Friday 15 October 1999. | specific where and when of experience

first person | I visited Judge Mary Pawlenty, a judge for whom I interned while in high

overview { school. Her calendar on the particular morning that I visited was a civil calendar consisting mainly of contested divorce hearings, although there were a number of default judgments that were included at the very beginning of the calendar. The majority of the default judgments involved landlords suing tenants for unpaid rent. Following the default judgment motions, Judge Pawlenty heard two cases. In the first case, the grandmother

and father of a one-year-old little girl were bringing a motion to amend the | chronological order

visitation rights of the father so that the grandmother could have visitation

rights. The defendant, the child's mother, was opposing the motion on the | details of what was grounds that the father did not have a stellar visitation record. She also felt | observed

that the grandmother could visit with the child during the father's

visitation times. The father's and grandmother's attorney admitted that

the father had not visited the child in two months, but beyond making

several excuses for this, argued that this would not factor into whether or

not the grandmother was allowed visitation. They argued that when the

mother and father had been on better terms, the grandmother had been

given visitation rights and that just because the mother and father were

no longer getting along, this should not preclude the grandmother from

offer insight from a conversation continuing her pattern of visitation. Judge Pawlenty took the matter | conversation <u>after</u> the under advisement, although she later said that she thought she would | specific observation allow the grandmother to have visitation.

first person

details of what was observed

2. The Case Study

The case study is an important research tool, and therefore writing assignment, in psychology, sociology, anthropology, and political science. Case studies are usually informative rather than persuasive. They present a problem or question and propose a solution or answer. Therefore, even though you are recording your observations, remove yourself from the writing and remain objective by using the third person rather than the first person.

There is a particular format to follow for case studies in most fields. With slight variations, this basic format includes: a statement of the problem being investigated; the background of the problem; the observations of the individual or group being studied; the conclusions, and the final recommendations for the future. In undergraduate courses, it is more likely that you will be asked to read, evaluate, and write a case study through research rather than field work.

*The following excerpt is part of a **case study** written by psychology major Angelica Bonacci. For this assignment, Angelica was asked to research and evaluate the case known as "The Man Who Mistook His Wife for a Hat."*

Patient Background: Dr. P. was an adult male referred to Dr. Sacks by his ophthalmologist. A well-respected musician, Dr. P. began his career as a singer and, at the time of observation, was a teacher at the local School of Music. Dr. P's problems were first observed while he interacted with his students. Often times, students would present themselves to Dr. P., but he would not recognize them as long as they remained silent. As soon as they verbally greeted Dr. P., he was able to recognize them and would interact with them normally. Thus, it appeared that Dr. P. did not have difficulty recognizing people per se, but he seemed unable to recognize faces. In addition, Dr. P. seemed to see faces in inanimate objects. For example, he often mistook water hydrants and parking meters for children, and attempted to engage doorknobs and furniture in conversation. Though the symptoms began almost three years prior to referral, Dr. P., and others, simply dismissed the oddities as jokes. His intelligence and musical abilities were as astute as ever, and no one, including Dr. P., thought there was anything physically wrong. Three years after the onset of the symptoms,

overview of case

chronological order of case

facts and details show close reading

Dr. P. was diagnosed with Type II (adult onset) diabetes. Dr. P. understood | diagnosis

that diabetes could affect his eyes, so he sought the opinion of an

ophthalmologist. After a detailed exam, the doctor concluded that Dr. P.'s

eyes were fine, but that there was "trouble with the visual parts of [the]

brain" (p. 8–9). The ophthalmologist recommended that Dr. P. consult a | direct
| citation
neurologist and referred him to Dr. Sacks.

After their first meeting, Dr. Sacks concluded that Dr. P. was of

extraordinary intelligence and showed no signs of dementia, or physical | conclusion of
| 1st part of
| case study
visual impairments, that could explain his confusion.

3. The Literature Review (also known as the Literature Survey in Natural Sciences)

The **literature review** is an important writing assignment for students because they not only learn and appreciate the past and present dialogue on a given topic, but they are also called upon to compile these materials in a succinct and organized fashion for the reader. By reading, summarizing, and analyzing scholarship, you demonstrate a basic understanding of the subject as well as an appreciation for the various critical approaches to that subject. Oftentimes, a literature review is a part of a larger proposal or report. You offer it as evidence that you have done the appropriate research before conducting your own inquiry on that or a similar topic.

The following excerpt comes from a graduate psychology paper in which the students, Victoria Fleming and Joyce Alexander, prepared the literature review as an introduction to their own study on the benefits of peer collaboration. Rather than specifically evaluate sources (as found in the bibliographic essay under humanities), the literature review is organized thematically.

introduce /   Cognitive strategy instruction, or the direct instruction of skills
subject

for learning, remembering, and monitoring, is believed to hold vast

potential for improving student learning, particularly vocabulary

learning, reading comprehension, and mathematical problem-solving
                                                         APA
abilities (Peterson & Swing, 1983). A growing body of research supports citation
                                                          style
overview of this assertion that direct strategy instruction can benefit students
supporting
  literature (Jacobs & Partis, 1987; Osman & Hannafin, 1992); Perkins & Salomon,

1988; Pressley & Van Meter, 1993; Graham & Harris, 1992; Stevens, Slavin, & Farnish, 1991).

move to explicate one of the studies in detail —— Peterson and Swing (1983) highlight both the importance of cognitive strategy instruction, as well as the practical limitations currently faced in its implementation. When children are taught cognitive strategies, they are likely to benefit in terms of recall and/or learning. However, teachers, who would be the logical choice for strategy instructors, are not typically trained to teach cognitive strategies. Even if they were, the time limitations and the high student:teacher ratio in most classrooms would make quality instruction difficult (Peterson & Swing, 1983).

4. The Proposal

Oftentimes, students are assigned proposals as the first step of larger research projects. Researching and writing a proposal helps clarify the purpose and narrow (or broaden) the scope of your final project. In a proposal, you convince your teacher that you have done enough preliminary research to know that your topic is significant and valuable. You also demonstrate that you will be investigating relevant sources and you intend to complete the project in a timely fashion.

Sometimes, you must send a letter of transmittal and résumé along with your proposal. If this is the case, see *Disciplines Section IV: Writing in Business* for details on these writing requirements.

The more thorough the proposal, the easier the setup for your final paper will be, as many sections are duplicated.

Most proposals will ask for some or all of the following sections. For all parts, except the cover sheet, use the headings as given here.

Cover Sheet

If required, the cover sheet includes your name, the title of your project, and the person or agency to which your proposal is submitted. It also provides a short title that concisely illuminates the topic at hand. Another line on the cover sheet may include the reason for the proposal—to fulfill a class requirement, to request funding, etc. Memo formats can also be used to convey all of this information.

Sample Cover Sheet:

The Adverse Effects of Teletubbies on
American Tots

Submitted to:
Dr. Jones

for:
Fulfillment of Course Requirement
in
Sociology 101

Submitted by:
Catherine Sullivan

November 1, 1999

Sample Memo Format:

To: Dr. Jones

From: Catherine Sullivan

Date: November 1, 1999

Subject: Proposal for a report on the adverse effects of Teletubbies
         on America's children for Sociology 101 course
         requirement

Abstract

On a separate page, the abstract provides a brief summary of your
proposal (see the sample paper at the end of this section for an
example of a social science abstract, and for an in-depth discussion of
abstracts, see *Section III: Writing in the Natural Sciences*).

Statement of Purpose

This short introduction (a paragraph or two) pinpoints the topic and
the goal of your work. Explain why you have chosen your topic and
what you hope to accomplish, and for whom. Prove that you have
carefully considered your topic and its value to a specific audience.

Background of the Problem

This section summarizes previous research and indicates the need for your specific investigation of this topic.

Rationale

If required, this section persuasively convinces the reader as to the importance of your research.

Statement of Qualification

If required, this section explains why you are the qualified person to conduct this research. It clearly states the unique qualifications you bring to the project.

Literature Review

This is a thorough section that establishes your credibility as a scholar by offering a brief survey of each source consulted thus far. It proves that what you want to investigate has yet to be done by someone else with the particular angle or perspective that you are bringing to it.

Research Methods

In this section, inform your reader how you intend to actually go about finding the answers or solutions to the problems you have presented in previous sections of the proposal. Describe exactly the research methods and materials you will use, demonstrating that they are sound and logical, as well as "doable."

Timetable

At the very least, the timetable shows how you intend to complete this project by the given deadline. A more detailed timetable looks more like a scheduled calendar in which you have mini-deadlines for various parts of your project: completion of compiling library research; dates for site visits and interviews; deadlines for distributing surveys and compiling data from collected surveys; draft date, etc.

Budget

If required, this section estimates any and all costs for completing the research. Make sure you do the necessary homework for this section. It is not a place for guesswork because your reader can and will make you stick to the numbers given here!

Conclusion

This section is a final, persuasive restatement of the importance of your project. This should be a confident, authoritative summary of why the proposal must be accepted.

5. The Journal Article

One of the best ways to truly become part of the ongoing dialogue in any given field is to submit an article on a particular subject to an appropriate scholarly journal. In the social sciences, this is encouraged at the undergraduate level as well as at the graduate level. When you have an article you feel is worthy of submission, ask your teacher for suggestions as to what journal might be interested in publishing it. Then, check that particular journal for details on entry requirements such as length and organization. Most journals are very particular about their manuscript requirements. It has been said that if you check 33 social science journals, you will get 32 different sets of requirements.

In general, however, the following make up the standard components of a journal article: *abstract, literature review, research methods, findings,* and *discussion.* The first three sections have been previously discussed under Proposals.

Findings

This section communicates the results of your research or study. These findings are often presented in tables, charts, and other such visual aids. The findings are objective and purely show the answers to questionnaires, surveys, observations, or test results.

Discussion

This section places the findings in relation to the findings of the other literature on this topic.

6. The Essay Exam

The essay exam is a common way for teachers to evaluate your overall comprehension of a variety of concepts. These are often taken in class, but sometimes take-home examinations are used as well. When you take an in-class essay exam, you must take the time to determine which question you can most successfully answer, then plan, organize, write, revise, and proofread—all in a limited amount of time!

WD Box 8 reviews some test-taking strategies for writing in-class essay exams.

Essay Exams

✓ **_Time Management:_** Read and understand the questions, and then determine how much time to spend on each section of the exam. For example, if you are required to write four essays in 60 minutes and they are weighed equally, you need to spend approximately 15 minutes on each question.

✓ **_Answer the Right Question:_** If you are given a number of questions to choose from, before you begin answering a particular question, make sure you can make three salient points to support your answer. If you can't, choose a different question.

✓ **_Answer the Question:_** This may seem obvious, but do exactly what the question asks. If you are asked to use a short story to explain a point, don't use a novel or a poem. If asked to define something, give a definition; don't argue about it. If the question asks you to do two things (trace and evaluate), make sure you do all things asked. A partial answer will not receive full credit.

✓ **_Pay Attention to Verbs:_** The question or prompt will provide the clue for what your answer should do: analyze, argue, classify, compare and contrast, defend, define, describe, discuss, evaluate, explain, summarize, trace, or refute. Do what is asked of you. See an overview of these terms in **WD Box 5**.

✓ **_Plan Your Answer:_** Take a few moments to make a short list of the major points you want to include in your answer. Without this list, students often go off on tangents and never complete their answers.

✓ **_Write Thoughtfully:_** Use an introduction (restating the question or prompt), paragraphs, and (if time) a brief conclusion. Demonstrate sound reasoning and an understanding of causal relationships; support your argument with evidence and specific details. Use proper grammar, spelling, and word usage.

✓ **_Proofread:_** Take a few moments to reread your answer. Omitting a key word such as "not" could completely alter your intended response and make your answer illogical at best and incorrect at worst.

The following **essay exam answer** was written by a student as part of an in-class midterm exam for a political science course.

The question read: *Define and discuss the history and ramifications of judicial review. Be sure to cite appropriate court cases.*

Judicial review is the power of the Supreme Court to make a law, from Congress or the states, null and void if it is deemed unconstitutional. Marbury vs. Madison was the first case to which the Supreme Court applied the concept of judicial review. This was a positive application of judicial review. One of the worst, if not the worst, applications of judicial review was the Dred Scott Case. The Supreme Court ruled that the Missouri Compromise was unconstitutional. This was an important flaming point and a pre-cursor to the Civil War.

Congress has ways to get around judicial review, however. First, and most unlikely, they could pass a Constitutional Amendment. This is extremely unlikely because of the lengthy and complex ratification process necessary to pass such an amendment. Second, Congress could re-write the bill so it would not be unconstitutional. This is much more common. Third, the order of the Supreme Court could be ignored and simply not implemented. This seems to be another common choice because the court has no way to implement or enforce their rulings. After all, there are still schools with the 10 Commandments hanging on the wall, and that was ruled unconstitutional many years ago.

Margin notes:
- define in a restatement of the question
- cite 1st case
- cite famous case
- use paragraphs for organization
- begin 2nd part of answer
- first, second, and third help move the paper along in a logical order
- concluding statement and citing specific example

✐ DOCUMENTATION IN THE SOCIAL SCIENCES

When writing papers in a social science course, it is your responsibility to clarify the guidelines for any given assignment. These include things such as length of the project, research requirements and/or restrictions, and documentation style.

Courses in the social sciences are the most consistent when it comes to standard documentation style as most follow APA guidelines.

American Psychological Association Sample Paper

The concept behind the APA format is simple: As the writer, you must clearly indicate all quotations, paraphrases, and summaries taken from outside sources each time they appear in your paper. On a separate page at the end of your paper labeled *References,* you then provide the complete bibliographic information of each source used. This page is prepared alphabetically.

For borrowed materials within your text, cite the author and year in the parenthetical indicator after the borrowed material. This is referred to as the "Name and Year" system of citation (also known as the Harvard system).

Only include the page numbers if the borrowed material is a direct quote. Whatever information you give in the signal phrase may be omitted from the citation following it. A comma is inserted between the author and the year, and if necessary, the year and the page number.

In one study (Bigner and Bozett, 1989), the most cited reason for why gay fathers come out to their children is the desire for their children to know who they really are. *[the names and year appear in a parenthetical reference]*

In Bigner and Bozett's study (1989), the most cited reason for why gay fathers come out to their children is the desire for their children to know who they really are. *[only the year is needed in the parenthetical reference as the names appear in the text itself]*

In Bigner and Bozett's 1989 study, the most cited reason for why gay fathers come out to their children is the desire for their children to know who they really are. *[no parenthetical reference is needed as all pertinent information was presented in the text]*

References

Bigner, J., & Bozett, F. (1989). Parenting by gay fathers. *Marriage and Family Review,* 14, 155-175.

⌨ **For online help with APA documentation, visit**
www.english.uiuc.edu/cws/wworkshop/bibliostyles
www.lib.usm.edu/~instruct/guides/ugindex
or
www.wisc.edu/writing/Handbook

✎ **STUDENT WRITING: AMERICAN PSYCHOLOGICAL ASSOCIATION SAMPLE PAPER**

The following pages are taken from a student educational psychology paper written using APA internal documentation style and a reference page. It was later published in the Journal of Experimental Child Psychology 67, 268–289 (1997).

Example of title page:

Peer Collaboration 1
The Benefits of Peer Collaboration on Strategy Use, Metacognitive Causal Attribution, and Recall
Victoria Fleming and Joyce M. Alexander
Dr. Kathy McMann February 1997

Abstract

This study examined the benefits of a peer collaborative activity on
cognitive strategy use and effectiveness, and on metacognitive
understanding of strategy use. Children's knowledge about the effectiveness
of the sorting strategy grouped them into lower and higher metacognitive
understanding. Treatment group triads, consisting of children with lower
and higher levels of metacognitive understanding, were given a collaborative
recall task. Results indicated that interaction with children working at a
higher level of metacognitive knowledge, in conjunction with directions to
explicitly discuss strategies, increased strategy use and induced higher
levels of metacognitive thinking in children who had been operating at
lower levels of metacognitive thinking. Overall, children's use of the sorting
and recall performance improved as a function of treatment group
membership. Implications for future research <u>are discussed</u>.

introduce
topic

introduce
method

introduce
results

passive voice
removes
writer from
overview

80

Benefits of Peer Collaboration on Strategy Use, Metacognitive Causal
Attribution, and Recall

Cognitive strategy instruction, or the direct instruction of skills for

learning, remembering, and monitoring, is believed to hold vast potential

for improving student learning, particularly vocabulary learning, reading

comprehension, and mathematical problem solving abilities (Peterson &

Swing, 1983). A growing body of research supports this assertion that

direct strategy instruction can benefit students (Jacobs & Paris, 1987;

Osman & Hannafin, 1992; Pressley & Van Meter, 1993; Sawyer, Graham,

& Harris, 1992).

Peterson and Swing (1983) highlight both the importance of cognitive

strategy instruction, as well as the practical limitations currently faced in

its implementation. When children are taught cognitive strategies, they are

likely to benefit in terms of recall and/or learning. However, teachers, who

would be the logical choice for strategy instructors, are not typically trained

to teach cognitive strategies. Even if they were, the time limitations and the

high student:teacher ratio in most classrooms would make quality

instruction difficult (Peterson & Swing, 1983).

Peer interventions can include students collaborating with, or directly

teaching, other students. Direct teaching often involves the assignment of

"tutor" and "tutee" roles to students. Although the assignment of these roles

might be useful in some situations, the threatening nature of that

arrangement, manifested in the tutee's sense of "incompetence, insecurity, indebtedness, and dependency" (DePaulo, Tan, Webb, Hoover, March, & Litowitz, 1989, p. 423), can make those labels synonymous with "smart" and "dumb" in the classroom. To avoid these negative connotations, peer collaborative activities involving group-oriented contingencies are often used (Slavin, 1987). These paradigms involve students simply working together to achieve a common goal, without the designated tutor/tutee labels. Research has demonstrated that such group-oriented contingencies often generate "collateral or untrained forms of peer management" (Borkowski, 1985, p. 54).

authors, date, and page # after exact/direct quotations

table label

TABLE 1

T Test Results on Phase I Variables

insert table that is discussed in text

	Treatment		Control			
	Mean	SD	Mean	SD	t	p
Metacognitive causal attribution	2.14	1.17	2.20	1.20	.25	.81
Item recall percentage	.58	.16	.61	.17	.95	.35
Overt strategy sophistication	3.25	1.50	3.28	1.74	.07	.94
General metacognitive knowledge	28.89	3.07	28.23	3.58	-.90	.37
Sorting during learning period	.47	.37	.53	.41	.77	.44

Questions were scored so that 3 points was the maximum credit for a total of 33 possible points (see the Appendix for the interview and scoring protocol). Interrater reliability was Kappa = .92. Discrepancies were resolved through discussion.

Appendix used for longer or intrusive information

RESULTS   heading

Phase I: Pre-treatment and Group Assignment   subheading

Random assignment of the matched pairs of subjects to treatment or control conditions, based on variables assessed in Phase I, was essential for interpreting Phase III outcomes. We wanted to ensure that all Phase I variables, including metacognitive causal attribution, number of items recalled on Trial 1 (spontaneous, non-prompted trial), overt strategy sophistication on Trial 1, and general metacognitive knowledge did not differ between the children assigned to treatment and control conditions.

As can be seen in Table 1, T tests run on the Phase I variables revealed

non-significant differences between the treatment and control groups

reference to table (See Table 1).

extra spacing between sections

Phase II: Treatment and Control Group Performance

In Phase II, children worked in triads, either collaboratively

(treatment) or side-by-side on individual tasks (control). Videotapes of

Phase II were coded for instances of: (1) metacognitive verbalizations, (2)

cognitive interactions, and (3) time-on-task. Two raters coded a random

sample (13%) of the tapes with 92% agreement. Discrepancies were

resolved through discussion. A single rater continued to rate the rest of

the tapes.

centered
REFERENCES | *all caps*
do not bold or underline

alphabetical listing,
last names only

Alexander. J.M. (1996, April). Metacognition and sorting strategy
development. Paper presented at the annual meeting of the American
Educational Research Association, New York, NY.

Alexander, J.M. & Schwanenflugel, P.J. (1994). Strategy regulation: The role
of intelligence, metacognitive attributions, and knowledge base.
Developmental Psychology, 30(5), 709-723.

Bjorklund, D.F., Thomas, B.E., & Ornstein, P.A. (1983). Developmental trends
in children's typicality judgments. *Behavior Research Methods and
Instrumentation*, 15, 350-356/

Blaye, A., Light, P., Joiner, R., & Sheldon, S. (1991). Collaboration as a
facilitator or planning and problem solving on a computer-based task.
British Journal of Developmental Psychology, 9, 471-483.

Borkowski, J.G. (1985). Signs of intelligence: Strategy generalizations and
metacognition. In S.R. Yussen (ed.). *The growth and reflection in
children* (pp. 105-144). New York: Academic Press.

Brown, A.L., Campoine, J.C., & Day, J.D. (1981). Learning to learn: On
training students to learn from texts. *Educational Researcher*, 10,
14-21.

Dimant, R.J., & Bearison, D.J. (1991). Development of formal reasoning
during successive peer interactions. *Developmental Psychology*,
27(2), 277-284.

DePaulo, B.M., Tang, J., Webb, W., Hoover, C., Marsh, K., & Litowitz, C. (1989).
Age differences in reactions to help in a peer tutoring context. *Child
Development*, 60, 423-439.

*hanging
indent*

*double-space
throughout
page*

*italicize
books
and
journals*

*only the
first word
of titles are
initial capped*

85

Duran, R.T., & Gauvain, M. (1993). The role of age versus in peer collaboration during joint planning. *Journal of Experimental Child Psychology*, 44, 227-242.

Duren, P.E., & Cherrington, A. (1992). The effects of cooperative group work versus independent practice on the learning of some problem-solving strategies. *School Science and Mathematics*, 92, 80-83.

Fabricius, W.V., & Cavalier, L. (1989). The role of causal theories about memory in young children's memory strategy choice. *Child Development*, 60, 298-308.

The following excerpt is taken from a student paper written for an International Relations course using APA internal documentation style and a reference page. The document design looks more like an expository essay than a report. No title page or formal abstract was required.

abbreviated title as running header

Bridget McCarte
Dr. Gratzia Smeall
PO 350
September 16, 1999

single-space
no title page
needed

In Pursuit of the Alternative Path

In light of recent trends in the Muslim world, many claim Islamic militancy is past its peak. Instead of fighting with blows, Islamists now exchange blows with Arab regimes in court (Dockser Marcus, 1999). Several other Islamists have discovered another peaceful path to victory—unifying one billion Muslims worldwide (Loeb, 1999)—in the business world (Dockser Marcus, 1999).

APA citation style

no headings or sub-divisions used

Even Osama bin Laden, a well-known leader of Islamic extremists, has demonstrated the value of pursuing such alternative paths to victory. With the approximately $300 million he inherited from his deceased father, bin Laden has built himself a very profitable network.

References

double-space

5 space indent each entry

Dockser, Marcus, Amy (1999). Crackdown on Terror Has Muslim Militants Trying New Strategies. *Violence and Terrorism*, Dunshkin/McGraw-Hill, Connecticut.

single-space

alphabetically list entries by authors' last names

Loeb, Vernon. The Man who Pulls the Terrorists' Strings. *Violence and Terrorism*, Dunshkin/McGraw-Hill, Connecticut.

double-space between entries

Peterson, Scott (1999). How Reporters Cheat Assassins in Algeria's War with Islamists. *Violence and Terrorism*, Dunshkin/McGraw-Hill, Connecticut.

Discipline Section III: Writing in the Natural Sciences

The natural and applied sciences encompass a variety of subjects, including botany, biology, chemistry, earth sciences (geology, climatology), environmental studies, engineering, genetics, mathematics, physics, and zoology. The foundation of these subjects is defined as "the branch of learning concerned with the study of nature and the physical world through the process of questioning, observing, experimenting, and theorizing known as the scientific method." The applied sciences concentrate on the basic systems and processes that create the phenomena of the natural world around us. Writing in the natural sciences must clearly articulate the questions being asked, the methods being used, and the conclusions being sought. The writing remains highly objective and unbiased. Its purpose is to inform, rarely to persuade.

RESEARCH SOURCES

The writing projects required in most of these subjects are usually the result of observations and experimental research. Results are then tabulated, displayed, and discussed at length. Literature searches, summaries, and reviews are also important research tools in these fields.

There are many sources of general information for the natural sciences, beginning with the commonly used *Science Citation Index.* For more specific reference sources, see the appropriate subject category provided here.

Titles followed by an asterisk (*) indicate that the source also comes in some sort of electronic format (website, CD-ROM, online database, etc.). Always check with your librarian to see what is available to you.

General Science

*Applied Science and Technology Index**
CRC Handbook of Chemistry and Physics
Current Contents
*General Science Index**
McGraw-Hill Encyclopedia of Science and Technology
Reference Sources in Science, Engineering, Medicine, and Agriculture
*Science Citation Index**

Scientific and Technical Information Sources
Van Nostrand's Scientific Encyclopedia*

Databases

BIO-SIS Previews
CASearch
SCISEARCH
Agricola
CAB Abstracts
CINAHL
Compendex
Environmental Route Net

NTIS
Inspec
MEDLINE
MATHSCI
Life Sciences Collection
CEOREF
Wildlife Review and Fisheries Review
World Patents Index

*Check with your librarian to see which databases are available at your library.

Chemistry

A Dictionary of Chemistry
Analytical Abstracts
Chemical Abstracts*
Chemical Technology*
Dictionary of Organic Compounds

Encyclopedia of Chemistry
Kirk-Othmer Encyclopedia of Chemical
   Technology
McGraw-Hill Encyclopedia of Chemistry

Engineering

Engineering Encyclopedia
Engineering Index*
Environment Abstracts*
Government Reports Announcements and Index (NTIS)*
HRIS Abstracts (Highway Engineering)
Pollution Abstracts
Selected Water Resources Abstracts*

Earth Sciences

Abstracts of North American Geology
Annotated Bibliography of Economic Geology
Bibliography and Index of Geology*
Bibliography of North American Geology*
Encyclopedia of Earth System Science

Geographical Abstracts
Geological Abstracts
Geophysical Abstracts
Guide to USGA Publications

Life Sciences

Grzimek's Animal Life Encyclopedia
Bibliography of Agriculture

Encyclopedia of the Biological Sciences
Encyclopedia of Environmental Biology

Cumulative Index to Nursing and
Allied Health Literature*
Biological Abstracts*
Biological and Agricultural Index*
Biology Digest*
A Dictionary of Genetics
Encyclopedia of Bioethics

Environment Abstracts Annual*
Hospital Literature Index
Index Medicus
International Dictionary of Medicine
and Biology
International Nursing Index
Zoological Record*

Mathematics

Computer and Control Abstracts*
Current Index to Statistics*
Encyclopedia of Mathematics and its Applications
Encyclopedia of Statistical Sciences

Encyclopedic Dictionary of Mathematics
Index to Mathematical Papers
Mathematical Reviews
Universal Encyclopedia of Mathematics

Physics

Astronomy and Astrophysics Abstracts
Encyclopedia of Physics
Encyclopedic Dictionary of Physics
Physics Abstracts*
Solid State and Superconductivity Abstracts*

Non-Library Sources

More than in any other discipline, the natural science students have ample
opportunities to get outside of the library and gather information. This is done
in an endless number of ways depending on the specific subject being studied.

WRITING EXPECTATIONS IN THE NATURAL SCIENCES

Assignments for writing in the natural sciences are based on the **scientific
method** of questioning, observing, experimenting, and theorizing. They will fall
into two categories: (1) reports of original research and (2) summaries of the
current discussion on specific topics. Usually, the audience for original research
reports would be teachers and other scientists in a particular field. The audience
for discussion papers would probably have a broader base.

The purpose for most natural science papers is to inform other scientists of your
research, experiments, and results. Therefore, use clear **language** so that other
interested scientists outside your specific field can easily understand your paper.
Use the passive voice rather than the active voice so that your focus remains on
what is occurring rather than who is performing the experiments. The first
person (I) is acceptable only when writing about your own experiments, and

try to avoid the second person as that commands or instructs your readers rather than informs them. Direct quotations are rare in science papers.

The style of this writing should generally be unemotional and authoritative, as established through credible and concrete evidence.

Keep in mind that most computer **spell-checks** are not fully equipped to handle the highly specialized language of the natural sciences. Therefore, it is your responsibility to double-check the spelling throughout your papers.

✐ ORGANIZATIONAL PATTERNS IN THE NATURAL SCIENCES

The natural sciences rely on very set patterns of organization and format to present their findings. These are according to each specific subject, so the pattern for a biology paper would not necessarily be appropriate for an engineering paper. Therefore, it is important that you clarify any writing guidelines in each of your natural science classes regarding organization and format.

The natural science paper is usually divided into four parts: introduction, methods and materials, results, and conclusion. Additional sections may be required according to the needs of your particular subject.

The aim of science writing is not just to relate established facts, but to argue them in a problem-solution format. Any given natural science assignment may also ask for standard patterns of organization found in other academic writing: analysis; cause/effect; compare/contrast; classification; response; problem/solution; and question/answer.

✐ DOCUMENT DESIGN BASICS FOR THE NATURAL SCIENCES

Margins and Line Spacing

The general **Document Design Basics** presented in this supplement regarding margins, fonts, and headings should be followed for most of your science courses. Double-space throughout the paper, and indicate new paragraphs by adding extra lines between the paragraphs rather than indenting the first word of each paragraph. As quotations are extremely rare in science papers, longer quotations are basically non-existent and no format guidelines exist for them.

Title Page

For your natural science papers, follow the format of the manual for that particular subject (see a listing of these under *Documentation in the Natural Sciences*).

The title of a natural science paper is extremely important and should be chosen very carefully. It must be a short, but descriptive, summary of the paper's subject. Use key words in your title because people find pertinent information on a given subject based on searching by key words or phrases. Therefore, if your paper is ever to be published, you want others interested in your topic to be able to find it!

Use a running title as part of your header (approximately one-half inch from the top of the page) on each page. This will be an abbreviated form of the title of the paper.

Example of title/first page of CBE paper:

Short Version of Title

1

Student's Name

Science Class 001

May 23, 1997

Longer Title:

Using Key Words and Phrases

Introduction

Use headings for the Introduction, Discussion, and Conclusion of your science paper. In the Discussion section, there may be subsections as well. Label them consistently and distinguish them from the major sections by the size, placement, or style of the headings. Try not to use third and fourth level headings. Paragraphs are indicated by extra spacing between paragraphs. The entire text (except for headings) should be left-flush; five space indents are not used.

Discussion

Some teachers in the natural sciences require that students begin each new section on a new page. However, that is now considered the exception rather than the rule, so always ask.

Visuals

For CBE papers, visuals are either tables or figures (including charts, graphs, illustrations, maps, and photographs). Statistical and mathematical copy can also presented in this way.

Do not use tables or figures unless repetitive data must be presented. Regurgitation of data just because you have it on hand makes your paper look longer but is not good science.

Tables are labeled with arabic numerals followed by a period. Place the label (also called the **caption**) centered above the table, with a brief, but informative, underlined (or italicized) title on the following line.

Any explanatory information appears immediately following the table, with superscript notations.

Example of CBE table:

TABLE 8.

Sizing Heavy-Duty Circuits

APPLIANCE	ELECTRICAL REQUIREMENTS	WIRE SIZE
Electric dryer	120/240 volts, up to 30 amps	#10
Electric water heater	240 volts, 20 to 30 amps	#12 for 20 amps or less
		#10 for 30 amps or less
Range	120/240 volts, up to 50 amps	Two #6 hot wires and a
		#8 neutral*
Refrigerator	120 volts, 15 to 20 amps	#12

*For smaller units, you may be able to use two #8 hot wires and a #10 neutral.

In the text, refer to the **tables** by their numbers. "As shown in Table 8 . . . ," but do not refer to tables "above" or "below" the text or by page numbers.

If the **table** (or figure) is **taken from another source** and not compiled by the student from his or her own data, the bibliographical information appears in a single-spaced note, and not on the References page at the end of the text.

*These recommendations are for standard, working appliances. (From Complete Guide to Home Repair (245), ed. Gerald M. Knox, 1980, Iowa: Meredith Corporation.)

Figures are labeled by the word "FIGURE" in all capital letters (or FIG.) and the consecutive arabic number followed by a period. Place this label below the figure. If needed, give a brief explanation, referred to as the **legend**. If this informational phrase or two uses more than one typed line, indent the first line by five spaces and single-space the entire legend. Figures have no titles other than this legend; therefore, the **legend** must be accurate yet concise.

Example of CBE figure:

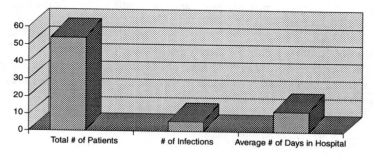

FIGURE 6. Incidence of hospital-acquired infections. (Courtesy of <u>Publish</u>. 57, 1983.)

In the text, refer to the **figures** by their numbers. "As shown in Figure 6 . . . ," but do not refer to figures "above" or "below" the text or by page numbers.

All **visuals** should be discussed within the text of the paper itself, and the visuals should be placed as close to this discussion as possible.

✐ ASSIGNMENTS IN THE NATURAL SCIENCES

Many of the writing assignments found in the natural science courses are common to the humanities and social sciences as well, such as case studies and proposals.

1. The Abstract
   Scientific reports usually begin with an abstract—a highly condensed precis for the convenience of the reader. Many times, readers only see the scientific abstract and not the entire paper, so make it good! There are two types of abstracts: descriptive and informative.

   The **descriptive abstract** (also known as an **indicative abstract**) offers a general overview of the content of the article or report. It is extremely short, usually only a few sentences. Because it offers few details and no conclusion, it is not the same thing as a summary. It may offer information about what the article or report discusses, but not how or why.

The **informative abstract** is more of a summary of the article or report that includes enough details so the reader could obtain essential information without ever reading the article or report itself. Think of an informative abstract as the table of contents in sentence form. It should be approximately two to five hundred words, in proper ratio to the actual article or report. Follow the same order in which the article presents the material, and include the purpose, method, results and conclusion—but only the most essential bits of each.

*The following scientific abstract is a **descriptive abstract** written by biology students to describe their study on "The Effect of Dehydroepiandrosterone on Blood Lymphoetye and Sperm Production in Adult Male Mice." Therefore, it is quite brief and reveals no methods or conclusions.*

Abstract

introduce topic | Dehydroepiandrosterone, DHEA, is an androgen that is produced by the adrenal gland. Research indicates that long-term treatment with DHEA results in decreased sperm production whereas both long-term and short- | background

purpose of this study | term DHEA treatment stimulates the immune system. The purpose of this study was to determine: (1) the effect of short-term DHEA treatment on immunity and sperm production in adult male mice and (2) to compare the effect of store-bought DHEA with DHEA purchased form Sigma Biochemical Company.

*The following scientific abstract is **an informative abstract** written by biology students and used to submit their study on "The Effect of Candida Albicans on White Blood Cell and Testicular Macrophage Production in Adult Mice" to a scientific conference.*

Abstract

topic | Candida albicans is a fungal pathogen that poses a threat to people with immune deficiencies. Therefore, this project examines the effect of *in vivo* infection of heat-killed C. albicans on immunity in healthy adult male and

summary | female mice. In order to determine whether the effect of C. albicans extends systemically to resident populations of macrophage at a distant site,

methods | testicular macrophage in male mice was examined. One million cells of C.

albicans were injected into each mouse through a subcutaneous injection, and control mice received a subcutaneous injection of PBS. After four days of treatment, blood was collected and identified with an Fc Receptor assay.

results | The outcomes indicate that in vivo injection with C. albicans results in an increase in total white blood cell production in male and female mice, and in increase in testicular macrophage in male mice. The increase in the number

conclusion | of testicular macrophage suggests a subcutaneous injection of C. albicans can affect systemic resident macrophage populations.

2. Abstract Summary

Unlike the abstract that you write about your own paper, an **abstract summary** reads more like a book review or annotated bibliography you might find in the humanities. The abstract summary provides a close examination of one particular source (usually a scientific study) in order to demonstrate that you understand the premise of the scientific inquiry, the methods used, and the conclusions both sought and found. Be very specific in the summary in order to show that you have not only read the original source, but also that you are fully aware of its implications on your own research and the scientific community at large.

The following abstract summary was written by a student in an Endocrinology course reviewing a study on "Heparin-Binding Epidermal Growth-Like Factor in Hippocampus."

The purpose of this study done by L. Opanashuk, R. Mark, J. Porter, D. Damm, M. Mattson, and K. Seroogy was to determine the expression of heparin-binding epidermal growth-like growth factor (HB-EGF) within rat | introduce the study being summarized | forebrains and whether this EGF receptor ligand had a neuroprotective role in response to kainate-induced seizures. The study used a variety of techniques such as Western analysis, Northern analysis, in situhybridization, and cultured hippocampal cell mediums to determine the role(s) of HB-EGF.

describes their methods | To start the study, the scientists had to determine where HB-EGF mRNA is expressed within the rat brains. They used a technique called in situ hybridization to monitor the production of HB-EGF mRNA production throughout development of the rat's hippocampus. Thin slices of forebrain were cut and hybridized with [^{36}S]-labeled HB-EGF cRNA probe. The hybridization was then visualized using autoradiography.

❧ OMITTED PARAGRAPHS ❧

describes
their
results

The study was successful in demonstrating that HB-EGF does have a neuroprotective role for hippocampal neurons against kainate toxicity. In situ hybridization and Western blot analysis revealed that both the HB-EGF mRNA and protein peaked around 24 hours after the kainate injection. The use of cultured hippocampal neurons in medium pretreated with HB-EGF protein demonstrated the inhibitory affect of HB-EGF on neuronal death caused by kainate-induced seizures.

3. The Laboratory Report

The most common assignment for a student in a science course will be the **lab report** (also known as test reports, experiment reports, or investigation reports). It is divided into standard sections that follow the stages of the scientific method: purpose, equipment, procedure, results, conclusions. Not every experiment requires each section, and some may need more, such as an abstract, reference list, or appendixes filled with tables, graphs, or charts. *The exact format of a lab report is usually defined by each course's textbook or manual.*

Whatever format you use, readers will expect your lab report to answer the following questions:

➤ why you performed the text—the reasons, goals, authorization
➤ how you performed the test—under what circumstances, controls, procedures, equipment
➤ what were the outcomes of the test—your results
➤ what implications or recommendations did you conclude from your test—what you learned, discovered, confirmed, disproved, or rejected

When writing papers in a natural science course, clarify the guidelines any given assignment. These include things such as length of assignment, research requirements and/or restrictions, and documentation style.

The documentation style changes for many of the natural sciences according to the subject. If you are majoring in one of these areas, you may want to invest in the subject's writing manual:

Biology:	CBE Style Manual (6th edition)
Chemistry:	The ACS Style Guide: A Manual for Authors and Editors (2nd edition)
Physics:	AIP Style Manual (4th edition)
Math:	Manual for Authors of Mathematical Papers (6th edition)

Engineering (The Institute for Electronics and Electrical Engineers) does not have its own writing manual, but two excellent sources are: (1) Effective Writing for Engineers, Managers, Scientists (2nd edition), ed. J.J. Tichy and Sylvia Fourdrinier and (2) How to Write and Publish Engineering Papers and Reports (3rd edition), ed. Herbert B. Michaelson.

Because some of the subject-specific natural science style manuals are very expensive (and often kept in the reference section of the library not to be taken out by students), you may prefer to invest in one of the general manuals for writing in the natural sciences, including: How to Write and Publish a Scientific Paper (3rd edition) by Robert A. Day and Science and Technical Writing: A Manual of Style by Philip Rubens.

📖 **For online help with CBE documentation, visit**
www.wisc.edu/writing/Handbook

Council of Biology Editors (CBE) Sample Paper

The CBE format is used for biology, botany, zoology, physiology, anatomy, and genetics. Therefore, the following sample paper for natural science uses CBE documentation style. CBE offers two formats: the author-date format (the Harvard system) similar to that used in APA style and the number-reference format similar to that used in CMS. The CBE version of the number-reference format varies considerably from the CMS format; therefore, that is the example shown here.

The logic behind the CBE documentation style is quite simple: As the writer, you must clearly indicate all quotations, paraphrases, and summaries taken from outside sources each time they appear in your paper and then, on a separate page at the end of your paper, provide a listing of each source with its complete bibliographic information.

You indicate borrowed materials within your paper with a number either in superscript or in parentheses following the borrowed materials. Your reader could then match this number with the corresponding number provided in the sequential listing on the separate "Reference" page.

Some fear that within 25 years, a society will begin sterilizing infants at

birth after technicians take a sample of the precursors of their eggs or

sperm (1). (or sperm[1])

Brief Title

15

References

1. Foote, C. Designing Better Humans. Sci Dig. 1987; 44: 131–132.

✐ Student Writing: Council of Biology Editors Sample Paper

The following paper is a biology student's research paper that uses CBE citations and reference page.

Investigating testicular regression and its link to immune function in a natural population of seasonal breeding deer mice.

repeat title from title page

heading | **Abstract**

topic | The purpose of the proposed research is to examine the seasonal fluctuations in reproductive and immune functions that occur in a natural population of seasonal breeding deer mice. This study is unique in that the majority of past studies have utilized laboratory-bred deer mice in place of a natural population. Cessation of breeding is one of the key coping strategies used by deer mice to survive the energy-demanding winters. In deer mice, there is a broad range of reproductive responses to environmental cues, such as photoperiod. During the short day of winter, some individuals undergo complete testicular regression, which is accompanied by a decrease

background

abbreviated title as running header

proposal of method

in testosterone production. Others do not exhibit testicular regression and are winter breeders. The proposed research will investigate 3-ß-hydroxysteroid dehydrogenase-isomerase (3ßHSD), an enzyme necessary for testosterone production, and its role in testicular regression. During the stressful conditions of winter, deer mice may also increase their chances of survival if individuals can invest more energy into their immunologic functions. This may be achieved more successfully if energy can be diverted from a different source, such as reproductive activities. In order to test this hypothesis in a natural population, the proposed research will examine the immune state in short day testicular regressed and non-regressed and long day deer mice.

Rationale and Objectives | heading

Animals inhabiting non-tropical latitudes must undergo physiological adaptations to meet the demands of potentially stressful seasonal conditions. The goal of the proposed research is to gain a better understanding of the seasonal fluctuations in reproductive and immune functions that occur in a natural population of seasonal breeding deer mice.

extra spacing between paragraphs

Cessation of breeding is one of the key coping strategies small rodents use to survive the energy-demanding winters (1). Typically, the cessation of reproductive function occurs during the fall and winter months in response to environmental cues, such as shorter photoperiod (2, 3). During the longer day length of spring and summer, reproductive responsiveness is restored. Interestingly, there appears to be a broad range of reproductive responses (2,4). In winter, about one-third of the males exhibit cessation of reproductive function, which includes testicular regression. Another one-third do not undergo testicular regression and are reproductively active during the winter. The remaining males exhibit an intermediate phenotype and are not winter breeders (2).

CBE citation style

The underlying physiological mechanisms(s)involved in mediating these differential reproductive responses remains unclear. Laboratory evidence suggests that the variations in reproductive phenotype in deer mice (Peromyscus maniculatus) may involve differences at the level of the hypothalamus, which in turn affects the testicular state (5). This proposal takes a new approach to investigating testicular regression in deer mice by examining the key steroidogenic enzyme, 3ß-hydroxysteroid dehydrogenase-isomerase (3ßHSD). The expression of 3ßHSD is absolutely essential for the synthesis of all biologically active hormones, including testosterone from the testes, mineralocorticoids and glucocorticoids from the adrenal glands, and estrogens and progestins from the ovaries. In humans, abnormalities in 3ßHSD are associated with pathologies such as congenital adrenal hyperplasia and hyperandrogenism (6). A great deal of research has centered on studying the regulation of 3ßHSD. However, the vast majority of this research has utilized in vitro cell culture or inbred lab rodents. To date, no studies have addressed the regulation of 3ßHSD in a natural mammalian population.

Examining testicular 3ßHSD in feral mice will provide key information on the 3ßHSD isoform family. It was previously reported that multiple isoforms of 3ßHSD protein are detectable in testes of inbred mice (7). The proposed research will address whether these isoforms are a product of the inbreeding process or if they also exist in the testes of feral deer mice. *The first objective is to test the hypothesis that multiple isoforms of 3ßHSD, detectable in inbred mice, are also detectable in feral mice.*

bold
italics for
emphasis

The proposed research also addresses a potential role of 3ßHSD in testicular regression. Previous research indicates that testosterone production is greatly reduced in testicular regressed mice (2). One possible explanation for reduced testosterone during regression is a decrease in one or more of the enzymes necessary for testosterone synthesis. Since 3ßHSD is essential for testosterone production by the testes, *the second objective is to test the hypothesis that 3ßHSD protein is decreased in testicular regressed mice compared to non-regressed mice during the short day of winter.*

The observed variation in reproductive phenotypes in the deer mice population may represent an important life history strategy for meeting the energy demands of winter. During the stressful conditions of winter, deer mice may increase their chances of survival if individuals can invest more energy into their immunologic functions. This may be achieved more successfully if energy can be diverted from a different source, such as reproductive activities. Laboratory studies support this theory that testicular regression and the cessation of breeding may provide rodents with needed energy to bolster their immune system during the short day of winter. One laboratory study reports that under short day conditions, testicular repressed deer mice have enhanced immune function, elevated splenocyte proliferation in response to a T-cell mitogen, when compared to non-regressed mice (8). However, this study only isolated one factor that occurs during the winter months—a shorter photoperiod. When studying natural populations, other factors must also be considered, such as temperature and food availability. Considering these other factors may explain the results of field studies that examine immune function. Natural populations generally exhibit reduced immune function during winter compared to spring and summer months, contradicting the laboratory studies. Taking into account both laboratory and field studies, we hypothesize that natural stressors of winter, such as lower temperature and reduced food availability, override the short day immulologic enhancement in testicular regressed deer mice. Therefore, our third objective is twofold. *First, we will test the hypothesis that all short day feral deer mice (both regressed and non-regressed) exhibit a decreased immune function compared to long day mice. Second, we will test the hypothesis that during the winter months regressed deer mice will exhibit an increased immune function compared to non-regressed mice.*

Preliminary Studies

no extra spacing
between sections

Data addressing the third objective regarding the immune function of long day deer mice was collected July–August, 1999. Feral deer mice (Peromyscus maniculatus) were captured using Sherman live traps in the long day of summer. The average paired testes weight: (mean 517 ± 187 mg) was within the normal range for long day non-regressed deer mice (5). Spleens were collected and a splenocyte proliferation assay was conducted (refer to method description). Consistent with reports using laboratory bred P.maniculatus (8), there was no detectable spleen proliferation in response to concavalin A within the long day deer mice (refer to graph on A7). However, the third objective of the proposed project is to determine difference in spleen proliferation between photoperiods, and not within a photoperiod. Therefore, the preliminary data will be compared to data collected this winter during a shorter photoperiod. Based on our hypothesis, we expect the absorbance readings for the splenocyte proliferation assay to be reduced in short day (both regressed and non-regressed) deer mice compared to long day deer mice.

Methods

sub-heading

Animal Collection

Deer mice (Peromyscus maniculatus) will be collected using Sherman live traps in Portage County, Wisconsin, during summer and winter months, 1999–2000. At least 10 sample mice of each phenotype (regressed and non-regressed) will be collected and the testes and spleen removed, placed on ice, and transported back to St. Norbert College for analysis and comparison to tissue collected from inbred mice (Balb-c strain).

Testicular Tissue Preparation

Decapsulated testes will be dispersed using a collagenase solution followed by mechanical dispersion. The dispersed tissue will be placed on ice to allow the sedimentation of seiniferous tubules. The tubules will be removed and the non-tubular cells collected by centribugation. Testicular cells will be lyseed in lysing buffer (1% sodium deoxycholate, 0.1% SDS, 0.8% mM Tris-HCL, pH 6.8) (9).

Western Analysis of 3ßHSD

The total protein concentration in lysed samples will be determined using a micro-BCA assay (10). Equivalent amounts of protein will be used for Western analysis to determine the isoforms and the amount of 3ßHSD immunoreactive mass protein in the samples for objectives one and two. A bovine 3ßHSD antiserum that was previously characterized and shown to recognize 3ßHSD in mice will be used for this research (11).

Measurement of Immune State Using a Splenocyte Proliferation Assay

Splenocyte proliferation will be determined using the T-cell mitogen concavalin A (Con A) using a previously described method with modification (8). Splenocytes will be separated from tissue by teasing cells out of capsule using two 27 gauge syringe needles. The separated cells will be suspended in 5.0 ml RPMI-1640 culture medium and centrifuged at 1200 RPM for seven minutes. Red blood cells are to be lysed with hypotonic shock and the splenocytes collected and washed several times using RPMI-1640 culture medium. Splenocyte counts and viability will be determined using a hemocytometer and trypan blue exclusion. Viable cells will be adjusted to 2×10^6 cells/ml by dilution with RPMI-1640 culture medium supplemented with 1M HEPES, 200 mM glutamine, 100 units/ml penicillin, 100 ug streptomycin, 5×10^{-2} M 2-mercaptoethanol and 5% fetal calf serum. Aliquots (50 ul) of cells will be added in duplicate to wells of a sterile flat-bottom 96 well culture plate. Con A will be diluted to concentrations of 40, 20, 10, 5, 2.5, 1.25, and 0.60 ug/ml and 50 ml of the mitogen will be added to the wells containing the splenocytes to a final volume of 100 ul per well. Culture plates will be incubated for 48 hours in 5% CO_2 at $37^{\circ}C$.

The optical density of each well will be determined with a microplate reader at 490 nm. The mean value for each set of duplicate wells will be calculated and used in the statistical analysis.

References

[handwritten margin note: double-space throughout page]

[handwritten margin note: entries are numbered and listed sequentially]

1. Millar J.S. 1984. Can. J. Zool. 63:1280-1284.

2. Blank J.L. and Desjardins C. 1986. Am J. Physiol. 250:R199-206.

3. Bronson F.H. 1987. In: Psychobiology of Reproductive Behavior; An Evolutionary Approach (Crews D.). Prentice Hall, Englewood Cliffs, JN, pp 204-230.

4. Turek F.W. and Campbell C.S. 1979. Biol. Reprod. 20:32-50.

5. Korytko A.I., Dluzen D.E., Blank J.L. 1997. Biol. Reprod. 56:617-624.

6. Mason J.L. 1993. Trends Endrocrinal Metabol. 4:199-202.

7. Keeny D.S., Naville D., Milewich L., Bartke A., Mason J.K. 1993. Endocrinology. 133:39-45.

8. Demas G.E., Klein D.L., Nelson R.J. 1996. J Comp Physiol A. 179:819-825.

9. Heggland S.J. and Stalvey J.R.D. 1996. Steroids. 61:309-326.

10. Smith P.K, Krohn R.I., Hermanson G.T., Mallia A.K., Gartner F.H., Provenzano M.D., Fujimoto E.N., Goeke N.M., Olson S.T., Kienk D.C. 1985. An Biochem. 150:76-85.

11. Perry J.E., Ishii-Ohba H., Stalvey J.R.D. 1991. Steroids 56:329-336.

Discipline Section IV: Writing in Business

Business writing is a highly specialized form of writing. Although many of the basic writing guidelines apply, there are enough unique aspects of writing for business to warrant its own section.

For most people and within most industries, writing impacts employees' careers—both positively and negatively. Effective business writing can help you find a job, perform your job better, and even help you earn promotions. Cover letters and letters of transmittal, which are forms of the standard business letter, play important roles of writing in the social and natural sciences as well.

RESEARCH SOURCES

Business writing requires some research, depending on the project. The most important thing to remember with business writing is that your information must be up to date. Your ideas and theories need to be considered in the economic climate for today and for tomorrow.

Titles followed by an asterisk (*) indicate that the source also comes in some sort of electronic format (website, CD-ROM, online database, etc.). Always check with your librarian to see what is available to you.

General Research Sources

Accountants' Index
Business Information Sources
Business Periodicals Index**
The Encyclopedia of Banking and Finance
The Encyclopedia of Management
Personnel Management Abstracts
The Wall Street Journal Index

✍ WRITING EXPECTATIONS FOR BUSINESS

Business writing should follow the three C's: Clear, Concise, and Correct.

The key to successful business writing is keeping your audience in mind at all times, determining your purpose for writing before you begin, presenting your ideas in a simple and organized manner, and editing and proofreading the final product carefully. In a business setting, you do not have time to waste when writing a document, and neither does the reader have time to waste when reading it. Therefore, your language should be lucid and precise, without industry jargon or fad "buzz" words. Your reader should always know exactly what is expected of him or her upon finishing your document.

✍ DOCUMENT DESIGN BASICS FOR BUSINESS

For most business writing, the general principles covered under **Document Design Basics** regarding margins, fonts, headings, and lists should be followed. Business writing generally follows MLA documentation style (even though it is considered part of the social sciences). Many companies and business writing courses rely on the *Gregg Manual of Style* as an additional reference book.

Line Spacing
Business writing is single-spaced rather than double-spaced. Most letters and other business documents follow the **block format**: left-flush (no paragraph indents) and double-spaced between paragraphs. Do not justify the text. A modified **block format** begins the date line and the closing at the center of the page and uses five space indents for paragraphing. The miscellaneous information (typist's initials, copy, etc.) at the bottom of the page is still left-flush.

Visuals
Tables are labeled with consecutive arabic numerals (suffixes are allowed if necessary). This should appear on a separate line above the table, centered, and followed by an appropriate, brief title using all capital letters. This title may appear on the line below or next to the label.

Use superscript letters or asterisks within the table to indicate **explanatory notes**, which are written directly below the table, single-spaced and adjusted to fit the width of the table or centered (if brief). If you are making a general commentary regarding the table rather than a specific point, place the word *Note:* followed by the information below the table.

Option #1: Using separate lines for label and title and a complete sentence for explanatory note. A general notation comments upon the entire table.

Table 13.3

NET PRICE ADJUSTMENTS

Item	Description	Net $ Added
Brake*	Class "B" coil, reverse mounted, anti-rattle hub	$7.38
Motor B987-23	Increased output torque	$3.29
Motor B987-25	.25 inch spacers used to set brakes off from motor end-cap	$.87

*There would be a one-time tooling charge of $1,500.00 to retool brake housing pressure plate.

Note: These adjustments were decided upon during the March 4 meeting.

Option #2: Using one line for label and title, adding a sub-title on a separate line rather than a general notation, and centering the explanatory note.

Table 13-3. Net Price Adjustments

Recommended Changes on March 4, 1998

Item	Description	Net $ Added
Brake*	Class "B" coil, reverse mounted, anti-rattle hub	$7.38
Motor B987-23	Increased output torque	$3.29
Motor B987-25	.25 inch spacers used to set brakes off from motor end-cap	$.87

*$1,500 charge to retool brake housing pressure plate.

Always place a **table** after it has been discussed in your text.

For **figures** (classified as any visual that is not a table), place the label below the figure, left-flush, all caps, followed by consecutive arabic numerals (suffixes are allowed if necessary) and an explanatory caption with a period, single-spaced.

FIGURE 3.c. This company logo will appear on all screen savers indicating poor weather conditions.

Documentation of Visuals

Following **figures and tables**, cite the source (single-spaced) of this information and permission to reprint it (if applicable) according to the documentation style you are using for your writing project, but be sure to include the title of the source, date of publication, and page number.

The following three examples are models for possible citation styles.

Source: Newsweek: February 27, 1995.

From Edward T. Hall, Beyond Culture (Garden City, NY: Anchor Press/Doubleday, 1976). Reprinted from Psychology Today, (July 1976): 67074. Reprinted by permission.

"An Employee Newsletter with Zing." Courtesy of Inc. Publications.

For most government publications (such as the U.S. Energy Information Administration), you do not need permission to reprint the table or figure used. Simply cite the source.

✐ ASSIGNMENTS IN BUSINESS

1. The Letter
   The business letter is the standard form of communication in the business world. There are many types of business letters: cover letters, complaint letters, bad news letters, good news letters, apologies, informative letters, confirmation letters, etc. No matter what the type of letter, follow these guidelines.

   Format. Use 8 1/2" X 11" paper of good quality, single-sided and single-spaced with one inch margins all the way around. Use the block format (left-flush) with double-spacing between paragraphs.

Letterhead. Most companies use their own letterhead. If you are writing on behalf of your company, use the company letterhead. If you are writing your own letter, it is easy to create your own letterhead using your computer software. At the top of the page, type your full name in a larger size font (14 or 16). Center it. Use a font that reflects your personality or business interest. Make it bold and/or italicized. Beneath that, type your address, then your telephone number in a slightly smaller font size:

Eveline B. Price
Fashion Consultant
8293 N. Prairie Circle
Milwaukee, WI 54222
414-964-9283

Depending on the software you have on your computer, you can be creative (within reason) when creating your return address.

If you would prefer not to use personalized letterhead, simply place your return address (omit your name) about one inch from the top of the first page. Spell out street names, but abbreviate the state using proper postal abbreviations and include the zip code. The date may be place two lines above this address.

Inside Address. Type the recipient's address two line spaces below your address. Include the person's full name (and title if appropriate), with his or her title on the line below, then the name of the department or division in the company, then the company name followed by the full street, city, and state address (including the zip code). If you do not have a person's name, omit that line and write to the title only (Personnel Director). If you have a full name, there is no reason to use the label "Attention" before the name.

Salutation. Double-space between the recipient's address and the salutation. If you use a reference line, space it evenly between the recipient's address and the salutation. The salutation begins with the word *Dear* and ends with a colon (:). Greet the reader the same way you would if you were speaking to him or her. Therefore, if you are on a first name basis, write *Dear Clare*. If you have a more formal relationship (or no relationship at all), write *Dear Ms. Reardon*. See **WD Box 8** for a listing of the most common salutation situations.

Paragraphs. Whenever possible, introduce the purpose of your letter in *the opening paragraph*. Set the tone as courteous, concerned, and competent.

Try not to give too many details in the opening paragraph. This opening simply tells the reader what the letter is about, creates the general tone of the message, and offers any reminders of previous communications.

The *follow-up paragraphs* should be approximately five to six typed lines long (not sentences). It is acceptable to occasionally use a one-sentence paragraph for effect. Even the shortest letters should be three paragraphs long: introduction, explanation or details of message, wrap-up. Within the follow-up paragraphs, put the most important information first. Do not bury it within long prose. For longer letters, headings may be appropriate, but don't overuse them.

After you have presented your message, provide a final *service paragraph*, one in which you reiterate the major point of your letter and then offer further assistance. It should provide the reader with a sense of closure and end on a positive note.

Closing. Before your signature and typed name, always end with a complimentary comment such as *Sincerely, Cordially, Yours truly, Respectfully yours*, or *Best regards*. If it is a two-word comment, only capitalize the first word.

Signature. Leave four blank lines between your closing and your typed name. If length is a factor, you may omit a line or two here. Sign your full name in this space, in ink—legibly.

Miscellaneous. If you are using a reference (subject) line, place it evenly between the recipient's address and the salutation. It should be left-flush and be written as *Subject:* followed by a concise summary of the topic of the letter. For more formal letters, the reference line is spaced evenly between the salutation and the opening paragraph.

Below the typed name and signature at the end of the letter, double-space and then include other notations, left-flush and single-spaced.

If the letter is typed by someone other than the person who signs the letter, the writer's initials are shown followed by the typist's initials.

The word *Enclosure* or *Enc.* indicates that additional materials mentioned in the letter are enclosed. You may also choose to verify the number of items enclosed or a description of the item(s)—Enclosures 4, Enc. 2, Enclosure: Application and envelope.

If the letter is sent in any way other than standard first-class mail, indicate this with the appropriate phrase: *By Federal Express, Via Facsimile, By certified mail, By messenger, By registered mail, Confirmation of fax sent on (date faxed), etc.*

If anyone other than the recipient named at the top of the letter is receiving a copy, type *cc:* or *Copy:* followed by the name(s) of the person (people) who will receive it.

These notations are all single-spaced, but for shorter letters you may double-space them for a more even page layout.

Writer's Typed Name

cm/jc (or cm:jc) indicates that Cynthia Manning wrote it and Jim Cook typed it
Enclosure: Check #123455 (or Enc.)
By certified mail
cc: Kathy Barnes (or Copy: or Copy to:)

WD Box 9 shows the courtesy salutations for the most common business writing situations.

```
WD
Box
9
```

Formal Greetings and Salutations

✓ To one person (name, gender, and preferred title preference known)
    Dear Mr. Close: Dear Ms. Kahler: Dear Dr. O'Meara:

✓ To one person (name known, gender unknown)
    Dear Pat Jacobs: Dear M.T. Felix: Dear Kim Swiatek:

✓ To one person (name unknown, gender known)
    Dear Madam: Dear Sir:

✓ To one person (name and gender unknown)
    Dear Sir or Madam: To Whom It May Concern:

✓ To one woman (preferred courtesy title unknown)
    Dear Ms. White: Dear Joanne White:

✓ To one man
    Dear Tom Brown: Dear Mr. Brown: Dear Tom:
    (the formality depends on your prior relationship)

✓ To two or more men
   Dear Mr. Lamar and Mr. Sloan:

✓ To two or more women
   Dear Mrs. Norton and Ms. Stiles: (use their preferred courtesy title)
   Dear Jenny Norton and Grace Stiles: (their preferred courtesy titles are unknown)

✓ To a woman and a man
   Dear Ms. Burns and Mr. Marconni:
   Dear Mr. and Mrs. Jackson:

✓ To several people
   Dear Mr. Andrews, Ms. Chan, Mr. Evans, and Dr. Noonan:
   Dear Friends: (colleagues, members, etc.)

✓ To an organization composed only of men
   Gentlemen:

✓ To an organization composed only of women
   Mesdames: or   Ladies:

✒ STUDENT WRITING: SAMPLE BUSINESS LETTER

NOSEEL ELECTRIC CORPORATION
P.O. BOX 43212, Port Washington, Wisconsin 53025 (262-299-9876)

about 2" from top

January 27, 1998 | *write out complete date*

| *2–4 lines*

Ms. Rebecca Molony | *always begin with an individual's name*
Sales Director
SEMCO
928 W. Bowling Green Ct.
Greenville, SC 29615

double-space

Dear Rebecca: *use the colon after the salutation*

Stacey Anderson and I would like to thank you for taking the time on Monday, January 26, 1998, to meet with us to discuss Noseel's capabilities and interest in becoming a full-scale motor supplier for SEMCO.   } *do not right justify*

Our technicians are completing the engineering modifications for motor N29382, and we should have those designs to you by February 3, at the very latest. | *single-space paragraphs*

114

At Noseel, we are looking forward to increasing your motor sales through our Profit Partnership Program, and we are certain Noseel will continue to be one of your most valued suppliers by providing you a quality product with available inventory at competitive prices.

Thank you again for your time on Monday and for your motor business in 1997. We look forward to a prosperous 1998 with your organization.

Sincerely, | closing

    | 2–4 lines for signature

Kevin Koweleski

kk:tm
Via fax on February 27, 1998 | delivery notation
Copy: Edmund Donne
        VP Sales

---

2. Résumé

A résumé is a brief, yet detailed, listing of your education, work experience, and qualifications to present to potential employers. Usually, you submit a résumé with a cover letter. If done well, these two documents can help you get an interview for a job. The cover letter introduces you to the reader and highlights certain qualifications using language similar to that found in the advertisement or job listing. The résumé should then persuade the reader that you should be interviewed for the job.

Most computer programs have outlines for résumés that you can simply personalize with your own information. In general, for applicants with little work experience, résumés should follow a chronological format: personal information; career objective statement (optional) education (beginning with your most recent degree); work experience (beginning with your most recent job); special skills or interests; and an offer to provide references. Try to get this on one page.

For applicants with five or more years of work experience, use a functional résumé with the following format: personal information; skills by appropriate category (management, fiscal, leadership, etc.); education; pertinent outside interests and activities; and an offer to provide references upon request. Try to get this on one or two pages.

Writing an Effective Cover Letter

✓ Follow the standard conventions for a business letter using quality bond paper. It may be colored paper, but use a soft, neutral color that reflects professionalism. Use the same quality paper for the cover letter, résumé, and envelope. Use a good printer and black ink.

✓ Consider the page layout and be generous with the margins and don't crowd the page.

✓ Try to send the letter to a specific person. Call the company for a name if the job advertisement does not give one.

✓ Sell yourself as an asset to the company. Instead of using all "I" clauses in the letter, incorporate what you will bring and could do to benefit their company.

✓ Organize the letter by short, clear paragraphs:

P1 = introduce the job you are applying for and how you heard about it.

P2 = relate your work experience to the new job echoing appropriate language from the job advertisement.

P3 = relate your education to the new job using appropriate language from the job advertisement that you have not used in the previous paragraph (P2 and P3 can be in reverse order as long as the strongest paragraph comes first.)

P4 = close with a reiteration of your major qualifications, ask for an interview or telephone call, explain when you are available for a follow-up conversation.

✓ Remember the three C's of business writing: Clear, Concise, and Correct. Convince the reader of your vast qualifications without using over-blown sentences or telegraphic clauses.

✓ Use formal and proper grammar. Use the spell check.

✓ Write your letter, then rewrite your letter. Let it sit for a day, and revise it one more time. First drafts are rarely the best drafts. Allow yourself time to improve this very important introduction of yourself to the potential employer.

✓ Edit and then proofread.

✓ Proofread again.

Sample cover letter:

MATTHEW J. MILLER
3102 GATEWAY COURT ◊ MEQUON, WISCONSIN 53092 ◊ (414) 242-6078
e-mail: mmiller@execpc.com

November 3, 1999

personalized letterhead created on a PC

Ms. Katherine Connor
Personnel Director
Image Consultants
P.O. Box 29838-7654
Grand Banks, NY 15532

Dear Ms. Connor:

Please accept the enclosed résumé as my application for the position of regional sales manager that was advertised on your website (www.image.com) on Tuesday, November 2, 1999. I am very familiar with Image Consultants and your national reputation as one of the top PR firms in the country. I realize this is a highly coveted position and the competition fierce; yet, I would appreciate it if you would take the time to read my résumé and consider me for this job as I truly believe I would be an energetic and creative addition to your team.

state the job, how you heard about it, and one "selling clause"

For the past eight years, I have been "learning the ropes" in the Public Relations field, moving up from the design team into corporate sales. Since joining the sales force, my background in art and design has proven invaluable to many of our corporate clients. I have become a skilled salesman at "closing the deal." As a hands-on account representative, I reassure my clients by following up on every aspect of their marketing or public relations project.

highlight work experience

Having taken the time to complete my MFA, I now bring a theoretical and academic background to the table that few sales people can match and few clients can dismiss. My education puts them at ease because they know they are hearing the very latest in marketing and promotional concepts.

highlight education

I would be honored to meet with you to discuss my qualifications for this position. I am available at your convenience on weekday afternoons. Thank you for giving me serious consideration for this job, and I look forward to hearing from you.

offer to meet at reader's convenience

Sincerely,

Matthew J. Miller

Enclosure: Résumé

Sample résumé (chronological):

MATTHEW J. MILLER
3102 GATEWAY COURT ◊ MEQUON, WISCONSIN 53092 ◊ (414) 242-6078
e-mail: mmiller@execpc.com

letterhead matches cover letter

CAREER OBJECTIVE

Looking for a management position in a national public relations firm that will utilize my sales experience and art and graphic design background to expand their corporate accounts in a fast-paced and competitive environment.

customize this for each job!

WORK EXPERIENCE | *bold-face for headings*

Milwaukee Design, Milwaukee, WI   May 1995–present

Account Representative. Responsible for bidding, maintaining, and closing six-figure sales contracts with new and existing corporate accounts. Doubled the number of accounts in my region in 18 months. Oversee the implementation of the final marketing concept and product, including budget and deadlines. Counsel corporate clients on marketing decisions. Conducted part of sales training program at national meeting.

use selling clauses and action verbs

Weston & Associates: Marketing Consultants, Milwaukee, WI Oct. 1991–May 1995

Sales Representative. Responsible for solicitation of new accounts through cold calling and presenting promotional and business materials. Assisted in conception and creation of national marketing pieces for Fortune 500 companies.

Big Music, Madison, WI   Feb. 1988–August 1990

Floor Display Designer. For three retail stores in the area, I designed and built promotional displays attracting customers and increasing sales.

EDUCATION

Milwaukee Institute of Design, Milwaukee, WI   Graduated March 1992

Masters of Fine Arts: Marketing Design

University of Wisconsin-Madison   Graduated December 1987

Bachelor of Arts: Graphic Design

OTHER RELEVANT SKILLS

Proficient in many graphic design computer software programs.

Fluent in Spanish.

Active member of National Guard.

only include activities that enhance your image

REFERENCES AVAILABLE UPON REQUEST

Sample résumé (functional):

MATTHEW J. MILLER
3102 GATEWAY COURT ◊ MEQUON, WISCONSIN 53092 ◊ (414) 242-6078
e-mail: mmiller@execpc.com

CAREER OBJECTIVE

Looking for a management position in a national public relations firm that will utilize my sales experience sales and art and graphic design background to expand their corporate accounts in a fast paced and competitive environment.

SALES and FINANCIAL SKILLS | *adapt the skill headings for each particular job*
- Bid and close six-figure sales contracts with new and existing corporate accounts.
- Forecast and maintain marketing and PR fiscal budgets.
- Increase the number of corporate accounts in my region by 100%.
- Cold calling prospective clients with a 42% success rate.
- Give presentations of promotional and business materials to prospective and existing clients.
- Oversee the implementation of the final marketing concept including budget and deadlines.

PUBLIC RELATIONS SKILLS
- Supervised and assisted activities of 10-person design team.
- Coordinated national marketing and promotional campaigns for Fortune 500 companies.
- Counseled corporate clients on marketing decisions.
- Conducted part of sales training program at national meeting.
- Chaired the Marketing Committee for the First Baptist Church.
- Active member of National Guard.

have at least 3 bullet points for each skill

GRAPHIC DESIGN SKILLS
- Designed and built promotional displays for retail store chain.
- Proficient and easily adapt to many graphic design computer software programs.
- Designed and coordinated national marketing campaigns, including "Hip to be Fit" and "Earth Day '96: Before It's Too Late."

WORK EXPERIENCE

simply list employers and job titles

Milwaukee Design, Milwaukee, WI   May 1995–present
   Account Representative
Weston & Associates: Marketing Consultants, Milwaukee, WI   Oct. 1991–May 1995
   Sales Representative
Big Music, Madison, WI   Feb. 1988–August 1991
   Floor Display Designer

EDUCATION

Milwaukee Institute of Design, Milwaukee, WI   Graduated March 1992
Masters of Fine Arts: Marketing Design

University of Wisconsin-Madison   Graduated December 1987
Bachelor of Arts: Graphic Design

REFERENCES AVAILABLE UPON REQUEST

3. The Memo

Because so much of business correspondence, particularly **internal correspondence**, occurs informally, memos are extremely important. Unfortunately, because memos occur internally, employees rarely take the time to carefully write them. Think of it this way: letters sent out to the public help establish your company's credentials and reputation for quality service and professionalism, but memos you write to your colleagues help establish your own credentials and reputation for quality service and professionalism.

Well-organized and written memos are an opportunity to "send the right message" to your co-workers and boss in more ways than one!

Memos are designed to deliver a small amount of information quickly. If you have a lot of information, you should not use this format.

Memos are in-house documents that can be sent through interoffice mail, fax, or even via e-mail. Certain verbs can remind you of the various **functions of memos**:

- ✓ *Announce*
- ✓ *Ask*
- ✓ *Explain*
- ✓ *Confirm*
- ✓ *Inform*
- ✓ *Provide*
- ✓ *Remind*
- ✓ *Suggest*
- ✓ *Summarize*
- ✓ *Test*

The **format of the memo** is usually determined according to the writing standards set by the company. Also, most computer software has a memo template that can be easily modified for your needs. However they are designed, memos are divided into two parts: the heading and the message.

The **heading** lists the reader(s), the writer(s), the subject, and the date.

The **message**, particularly a complicated or multi-faceted one, follows this pattern:

> *An Introduction* presents the problem (procedure, question, policy, etc.), any background information, and the intent of memo.

A Discussion of the topic offers precise details of who and what is involved, when and where something will occur, how something will occur, and why.

A Conclusion asks the reader for input or questions, requests that reply by a specific date, and offers specific recommendations to which the reader can respond.

Sample memo:

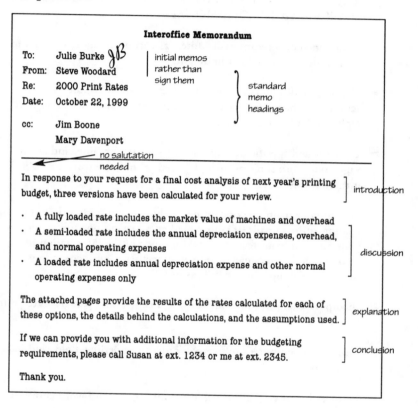

Interoffice Memorandum

To: Julie Burke   ⟨ *initial memos rather than sign them* ⟩
From: Steve Woodard
Re: 2000 Print Rates   *standard memo headings*
Date: October 22, 1999

cc: Jim Boone
         Mary Davenport

— *no salutation needed*

In response to your request for a final cost analysis of next year's printing budget, three versions have been calculated for your review.   *introduction*

- A fully loaded rate includes the market value of machines and overhead
- A semi-loaded rate includes the annual depreciation expenses, overhead, and normal operating expenses   *discussion*
- A loaded rate includes annual depreciation expense and other normal operating expenses only

The attached pages provide the results of the rates calculated for each of these options, the details behind the calculations, and the assumptions used.   *explanation*

If we can provide you with additional information for the budgeting requirements, please call Susan at ext. 1234 or me at ext. 2345.   *conclusion*

Thank you.

4. The E-mail.

You should consider e-mails as memos waiting to be printed. Therefore, they are leaving a paper trail of your writing skills that must be as professional as possible. When e-mails first became popular, there were no set rules or guidelines to follow, and many people picked up some lazy writing habits. Don't let this happen to you! Informal internal correspondence is not a free pass for sloppy writing or thinking. Try to use complete sentences, proper grammar, and remember to use greetings in your e-mails. They don't have to be formal, but just as you would never pick up the phone and start speaking without saying hello first, don't just jump into your message in an e-mail.

Format and "netiquette":

- ➤ DO NOT SEND MESSAGES IN ALL CAPITAL LETTERS. THIS "SHOUTING" TECHNIQUE MAKES IT DIFFICULT FOR YOUR READERS, AND THE HARD COPY OF YOUR MESSAGE WILL LOOK VERY UNPROFESSIONAL.

- ➤ Always include a return mail address as part of the signature, saving your reader the trouble of finding it.

- ➤ Use specific deadlines as the phrase "let me know" is not a call to action. Tell the reader exactly what you need him or her to do (call, reply, send a form, nothing).

- ➤ Use clear and specific descriptions for your subject line, and avoid vague one-word subjects such as "meeting" or "new software." Yet, keep it three words or less.

- ➤ Present your main message immediately as many readers do not bother reading entire e-mails. If your e-mail goes beyond one full screen on your monitor, your reader may skim much of the information in the second half of the e-mail or miss it altogether. Consider sending a memo or making a phone call instead.

- ➤ Incorporate an introduction, body, and concluding paragraph to your message.

- ➤ Learn your computer's software in order to underline, bold, and italicize for emphasis.

- ➤ Proofread your e-mail for spelling, punctuation, and word choice. Use the spell-check if you have one.

- ➤ Be careful with the body language references known as "emoticons" (smiley faces, frowns, kisses, etc.).

- ➤ Give a full reply when responding to a request, even if you are tempted to write a curt one or two word answer.

Confidentiality and Ethics of E-mails

Privacy is one of the greatest concerns with electronic mail in the business world today. The 1986 Electronic Communications Privacy Act (ECPA) prohibits phone and dataline taps with two exceptions: law enforcement agencies and employers. The company that owns the e-mail system is legally allowed to search the company mailboxes. Beware—big brother could be reading.

Observe the following guidelines to help protect confidential and sensitive information:

✓ Never "vent" in an e-mail. Do not attack your company, your boss, a co-worker, or even the competition in an e-mail.

✓ Do not gossip online!

✓ Send only the information requested. Not only does this ensure that your e-mail will be concise, but it helps lower the risk of divulging confidential information.

✓ Send nothing through the e-mail that you wouldn't want posted on the company bulletin board. Many Internet romances have been exposed through e-mails that accidentally went to incorrect recipients.

✓ If attaching documents, check for copyright infringements.

✓ If you want to distribute or publish something that someone has sent you, you must let the original sender of the material know your intentions.

✓ Do not change the wording of a message that you are simply supposed to read and forward.

✓ Avoid *"flaming"* e-mails that verbally attack, insult, or mock your e-mail reader. A flaming message will hurt you and your company and could even result in charges of libel against you and/or your employer.

Sample of a bad e-mail:

need
salutation ———

sloppy

Need phone # for Dr. peters in Beaver Falls Penn. 724-298-8736 is out of order no luck

on the internet or dir assistance   poor grammar

Let me no his new # if ya got it—

no — Wendy   slang

unclear where this
number came from

thank you or return address

Sample of a good e-mail:

Hi, Ted, — greeting

I am trying to order an application for Dr. Peters in Beaver Falls, PA, but the phone number listed in his file (724-298-8736) is no longer in service. } intro and clear explanation

I tried both the Internet and Directory Assistance—no luck so far!

Could you please contact me by the end of work tomorrow (Friday, Oct. 8) with either a current telephone number or a lead on how I might find it. } specific call to action

Thanks, Wendy
ext. 3876 } polite closing

5. The Short and Long Report

Short reports can include: sales reports, progress reports, trip reports, test reports, and incident reports. (Specific industries may require others such as inventory reports, feasibility reports, operations reports, etc.) Because they are brief, short reports can be presented in a memo or even e-mail format. Most companies have their own format for their standard reports. Also, the timetable of short reports is usually determined by the company. You could be asked to write them daily, weekly, bi-weekly, or monthly. Obviously, the time frame affects the depth and length of the writing.

Whatever these specific requirements, keep the following guidelines in mind when writing any type of short report:

✓ Do the necessary research to make the report worthwhile (vague reports are useless)

✓ Consider how your reader uses the report (write based on this)

✓ Report the facts objectively, truthfully, accurately, and ethically (avoid guesswork, impressions, assumptions, and unsubstantiated opinions)

✓ Use the company report forms, but make them reader-friendly by providing headings, white space, bullet points, and any necessary visuals (make sure the report never looks cluttered, cramped, or distracts from the message)

✓ Follow the basic rules of writing—clear, concise, and correct (avoid redundancies and wordiness in reports)

✓ Organize the report—purpose, findings, conclusions, and recommendations

Example of short report in memo format:

Memorandum

TO: Joe Larson
        Shipping & Receiving Manager

FROM: Dagmar Goldman   standard
        Account Executive   memo
                               format
DATE: January 8, 1999

RE: Packaging of glass mugs

---

use of
headings

Description of Problem

On Tuesday, January 5, 1999, a package of glass mugs was hand-delivered to us by an irate retail customer. She was returning it because all the mugs had been broken during shipment. We replaced her mugs immediately, apologized for the inconvenience, and proceeded to examine the box and its contents.

After a thorough evaluation, I found the box was improperly packaged. The wrong type of string was used to wrap the contents, allowing them to shift during shipment, and the outside of the carton was incorrectly sealed. In addition, the box lacked the required structural integrity.

As a result of the improper packaging, all the glass mugs were broken during the shipment, which was only five miles from our factory. The value of the contents of the box was listed at $1,375.

Causes of Problem

Proper procedures were not followed to ensure preservation of the glass mugs. The incorrect type of string allowed the mugs to shift during shipment. Also, no Styrofoam was placed in the box to separate and support the glassware and to help uphold the structural integrity of the box. Instead, tissue had been used.

When asked, the packing personnel said they were out of the proper type of string (it had been ordered, but never arrived), and Styrofoam was no longer being used due to high costs.

Recommendations

The best way to ship glassware is to reinforce the corners of the box with Styrofoam padding. Smaller pieces of this padding should also be placed between the individual pieces of glassware. The carton should then be tied tightly with the correct type of packaging string.

I personally ordered (and already received) more packaging string, and found a less expensive supplier for Styrofoam padding, which is now being used.

Long reports are much more than extended versions of short reports. They differ in topic, scope, format, and even audience and usefulness. A long report could begin with a proposal (see The Proposal under *Section II: Writing in the Social Sciences*) to your boss or a committee asking for permission to take the time (and money) to conduct the necessary work to compile a long report. A long report will provide an in-depth study of a problem, idea, or situation. It begins by introducing the history of the topic and provides background information relevant to the discussion. It then examines well-researched options, plans, and opinions. This could include library research, on-site visits, interviews, surveys, or tests. It also provides extensive information from experts regarding the topic in order to provide a final recommendation.

Format

The scope of the long report is too broad for a memo or e-mail format. The standard long report includes all or some of the following sections, which can be divided into three parts: front matter, report, and back matter.

Front Matter. This portion of your report includes everything preceding the actual text of your report.

- ✓ **Letter of transmittal.** This is a cover letter that states the purpose, scope, and recommendations of the report. If your report is being done for a class, the letter should state this as part of its purpose.
- ✓ **Title page.** The format for this page does not follow MLA, CMS, or APA guidelines exactly, but is more of a hybrid of all of them. The title is in all caps, but if there is a second part to the title following a colon, use both upper and lower case for it (MAIN TITLE: Subtitle That Offers Further Detail). This is centered and approximately three inches from the top of the page. Beneath this include the company or person for whom the report was prepared, your name as the writer, and the date. If it is for a class, indicate the teacher's name and the course name and number as well.
- ✓ **Table of contents.** This page tells the reader the contents of the report; specifically, it gives the page numbers and shows how you organized the report. Include front matter components in the table of contents, but never list the contents page itself, the letter of transmittal, or the title page.
- ✓ **List of Illustrations.** *If applicable*, this lists where all the visuals can be found in your report.
- ✓ **Abstract.** An abstract presents a brief overview of the problem and conclusions. All abstracts share two characteristics: they never use the word "I" and they never use footnotes (for more details, see The Abstract under *Section III: Writing in the Natural Sciences*).

The Introduction

Background. To understand why your topic is significant and hence worthy of study, readers need to know about its history. This history may include information such as who was originally involved, when, and where; how someone was affected by the issue; what opinions have been expressed on the issue, and what the implications of your study are or could be.

Problem. Identify the problem or issue that led you to write the report. Since this determines everything you write about, your statement of the issue must be clear and precise. It should, however, be restricted to a few sentences.

Purpose Statement. The purpose statement, crucial to the success of the report, tells readers why you wrote the report and what you hope to accomplish or prove. Indicate how such information you compile might be useful to a specific audience, company, or group. Like the problem statement, the purpose statement does not have to be long or complex.

Scope. This section informs the readers about the specific limits— number and type of issues, times, money, locations, personnel— you have placed on your investigation.

The Discussion

This is the longest and most substantial part of your report. The discussion supplies readers with statistical information, details, and descriptions, as well as interpretations and comments from the experts whose work you consulted as part of your research.

Plan this section carefully. Separate the material in the body of your report into meaningful parts to make sure that you identify the major issues as well as sub-issues. Use **headings** to help your reader identify major sections quickly. Use them consistently throughout the report and make them easy to follow. These organizational headings should allow a certain amount of skimming as well. The headings are, of course, presented in the Table of Contents.

In addition to headings, use **transitions** to guide your discussion from one point to the next. At the beginning of each major section, tell readers what they will find in that section and why. Summary sentences at the end of a section then remind readers where they have been and prepare them for where they are going.

The Conclusion
This section ties it all together for the reader by presenting the findings of your report. Your conclusions should be based on the information and the documentation presented in the discussion of your report. Do not contradict anything you have presented in your own report, and do not go off on tangents that cannot be substantiated by your own data. Poorly written conclusions can do more harm than good!

Recommendations
For a strictly academic report, this section may be omitted; however, for other business or scientific reports, the recommendation can be considered the most important part of the report. The recommendation section tells the readers what should be done with the findings recorded in the conclusion. It answers the readers' most basic question: So what?

Back Matter. As implied by its title, this material is the supporting data that follows the bulk of your paper. If you had included it in the discussion, it would bog the reader down, yet it still provides vital information.

✓ *Glossary.* This provides an alphabetical listing of any specialized vocabulary with definitions. Consider the needs of your audience when deciding whether or not to include a glossary.

✓ *References.* List all sources cited in your report—written, oral, video, electronic, internet—in this section. Ask your employer or teacher how this information should be cited internally and listed in the **Back Matter**. Options usually include following MLA, APA, or *The Chicago Manual of Style*, all of which are presented elsewhere in this supplement.

✓ *Appendix (Appendices).* This section contains all the supporting materials for the report—tables and charts too long for the discussion section, sample questionnaires, budgets, estimates, correspondence, case histories, transcripts of telephone calls, etc. Group similar items together in the appendix.

Excerpts from long report using MLA documentation style:

FLEXTIME:
An Alternative to Fixed
Work Schedules

Duyen Bagwell
May 1, 1997

Business Management 295
Professor Jay Jacobs

Table of Contents

Excerpts from long report using MLA documentation style:

For this front matter material, page numbers appear in the form of roman numerals, centered, at the bottom of each page.

LIST OF ILLUSTRATIONS

ABSTRACT

Flexible working practices are on the rise in many major corporations. The most common form of flexible working practice is FlexTime. FlexTime involves replacing traditional fixed work schedules with an alternative practice that allows employees to choose their arrival and departure times. FlexTime can affect many aspects of the work experience by allowing employees to adapt their own work schedules. FlexTime influences employee attitudes though increased participation in decision making. FlexTime also enhances group cohesiveness, as employees must cooperate to maintain work processes. In addition to improving quality of life, FlexTime improves the fit between employee work and personal domains. Despite its many advantages, FlexTime presents some concerns, as well. However, the disadvantages for most companies studied for this paper were few. An understanding of the advantages and disadvantages of FlexTime is important to organizations considering it as an alternative scheduling option in order to achieve increased productivity. This report will provide background information and recommendations for those companies considering implementation of FlexTime.

Excerpts from long report using MLA documentation style:

INTRODUCTION

Background

With the trend toward working outside the home after the mid-1800s, fixed work schedules became the common scheduling practices of many businesses. After the 1960s, however, businesses were looking to establish a more flexible culture that employees would accept during times of economic changes. In 1967, FlexTime was introduced to alleviate traffic problems faced by employees of a German aerospace company. Many businesses recognized the alleviation of traffic problems as only one of the many benefits of this new scheduling, and the concept spread quickly throughout Germany and Western Europe. The United States slowly adopted FlexTime shortly thereafter (Ronen 372).

✍ Omitted Paragraphs ✍

Problem

Retention has become a major reason for workplace flexibility programs. Many businesses are turning to FlexTime because of low unemployment levels and high employee turn-over. The shortage of labor and the desire of employers to attract quality individuals are key reasons for businesses to at least consider FlexTime. It provides a means by which they can retain effective employees or recruit new ones (Graham).

Bagwell 12

Works Cited

Folkard, Simon and Timothy H. Monk. Hours of Work: Temporal Factors in Work-Scheduling. New York: John Welsy & Sons Ltd., 1985.

Graham, Baxter W. "The Business Argument for Flexibility." HR Magazine. May 1996: 2.

Ronen, Simcha. Alternative Work Schedules. Homewood: Dow Jones-Irwin, 1984.

6. Collaborative Writing

Teamwork is an important part of most businesses, and when it comes to collaborative writing, teamwork is essential. **Collaborative writing** benefits the employees involved as well as the company because it uses the diverse talents of the individuals involved, it can save time, it allows for more thoroughness and productive feedback, it encourages company morale, and it responds better to customers' needs. All of this is only achieved, however, if the collaborative writing process is efficient and effective. The team must cooperate, corroborate, and conform. There are a number of collaborative writing models you may choose from depending on the scope and nature of the writing project.

Cooperative Writing

This form of collaboration has you write a draft and show it to other people for feedback. Based on that feedback, you revise your draft. There is interaction between you and anyone who has read your draft, but ultimately, the responsibility of the end product lies with you. If you are asked to provide the feedback in cooperative writing, try to remain objective and critique the clarity of the message, the effectiveness of the message, and the correctness of the message. Don't let the document become a battleground for egos and personal agendas. Avoid changing someone's language unless it is incorrect or negatively impacts the writing. Avoid revising sentence structure unless it is awkward or incorrectly presenting information.

Sequential Writing

This form of collaboration has individuals each write a portion of a larger writing project. These sections do not overlap. The individuals may help each other with drafts and feedback, but not necessarily. One person, usually the strongest writer, then coordinates the final project.

Functional Writing

This form of collaboration divides the responsibilities of a writing project according to the strengths of the team members. Therefore, one person may do all research and no writing, while another coordinates the meeting schedules, deadlines, and progress reports, while a third prepares the visuals. This form demands a lot of group interaction and trust that all members are doing their jobs.

Integrated Writing

This form of collaboration gives all team members a vital role in every aspect of the project. This form demands intense group interaction and coordination as all individuals share the responsibility for the entire document. This includes compiling, editing, and revising the final version.

Cowriting

This form of collaboration has all team members write all the drafts, word for word, together. They all work on the same document at the same time, either in a meeting or through their company's computer system. This is a labor-intensive form of team work and is only cost-effective and practical for shorter writing projects.

See **WD Box 12** for tips on how to organize and delegate within your collaborative writing project.

```
WD
Box
12
```

Guidelines for Successful Collaborative Writing

1. **Establish rapport with team members.** Take the time to get to know each other, your schedules, and your strengths and weaknesses to establish an environment conducive to sharing and working together.

2. **Think as a team.** Remember that the team succeeds together or fails together and there is no place for egotism or favoritism.

3. **Establish guidelines.** Make sure all team members have the same goal for the project, and the group should discuss the objectives, audience, scope, format, and overall expectations before any delegating, researching, or writing occurs.

4. **Organize the team.**

    Is there a group leader? Who should it be? What are the leader's responsibilities, and how far reaching will his or her authority be as the "final say" on various decisions?

    How will the group communicate with management during the project? How often?

    Will there be a secretary or someone to record and distribute minutes, documents, or updates following all meetings?

5. **Identify individuals' responsibilities.** Try to delegate the division of labor based on people's talents and areas of expertise so that individuals feel comfortable with their assigned duties.

6. **Make a calendar.** Pre-set meetings and deadlines so there are minimal excuses for missing them. But don't forget that projects usually take longer than expected, so be ready to be flexible.

7. **Set a documentation style.** Select the software that will be used as well as the documentation style so that merging various sections of writing will be easier and there will be less editing to do.

8. **Provide useful feedback on writing.** Decide if this feedback will be written on drafts or face-to-face. Either way, be specific with suggestions and generous with positive comments. Avoid critiquing personal style if possible.

✐ DOCUMENTATION IN BUSINESS WRITING

Similar to writing in the humanities, social sciences, and natural sciences, documentation plays an important role in business writing. It tells your reader that you have done your homework—consulted experts, read the latest articles, checked the pertinent websites. Providing the documentation for this research is not only a courtesy to your reader, but it is an ethical requirement to acknowledge borrowed materials.

Business writing is usually documented with either MLA or APA style.

For cover letters and résumés, there are a number of resources that can help you create a strong impression on perspective employers:

<u>The Résumé Reference Book</u> by Howard Lauther (1990)

<u>The Résumé Writer's Handbook</u> by Michael Holley Smith (1993)

<u>High Impact Résumés and Letters</u> by Ronald L. Krannich

<u>Résumé Reference Manual</u> by Carl Gosmann (1993)

 # References

Anderson, Paul V. <u>Technical Communication: A Reader-Centered Approach</u> (4th edition). Harcourt Brace: 1998.

Day, Robert A. <u>How to Write and Publish a Scientific Paper</u> (2nd edition). ISI Press: 1983.

Fulwiler, Toby and Alan R. Hayakawa. <u>The College Writer's Reference</u> (2nd edition). Prentice-Hall: 1999.

Geever, Jane C. and Patricia McNeil. <u>Guide to Proposal Writing</u>. Foundation Center: 1997.

Gregory, Hamilton. <u>Public Speaking for College & Career</u> (4th edition). McGraw-Hill: 1996.

Goldstien, Norm. Ed. <u>The Associated Press Stylebook and Libel Manual</u>. Perseus Books: 1998.

Holoman, D. Kern. <u>Writing About Music</u>. U of CA Press: 1988,

Kirszner, Laurie G. and Stephen R. Mandell. <u>The Holt Handbook</u> (5th edition). Harcourt Brace: 1999.

Kolin, Philip C. <u>Successful Writing at Work</u>. Houghton Mifflin Company: 1998.

<u>MLA Handbook for Writers of Research Papers</u> (5th edition). MLA: 1998.

<u>Publication Manual of the American Psychological Association</u> (4th edition). APA: 1994.

Sprague, Jo and Douglas Stuart. <u>The Speaker's Handbook</u>. Harcourt Brace: 1996.

<u>The Chicago Manual of Style</u> (14th edition). U of Chicago Press: 1993.

Turabian, Kate L. <u>A Manual for Writers of Term Papers, Theses, and Dissertations</u> (6th edition). U of Chicago Press: 1996.